In-Fisherman
PRESENTS *Cooking*
FRESHWATER FISH
By Chef Lucia Watson

In-Fisherman Presents . . .

COOKING FRESHWATER FISH

Publisher *Steve Hoffman*

Editor In Chief *Doug Stange*

Art Director *Chuck Beasley*

Copy Editor *Kathy Callaway*

Editorial Assistant *Claudette Kitzman*

Production Assistants *Amy Jackson and Jan Schneider*

Staff Photographer *Jeff Simpson*

Project Author *Lucia Watson*

Project Photographer *Chuck Nelson*

COOKING FRESHWATER FISH

First Edition

ISBN: 1-892947-72-2

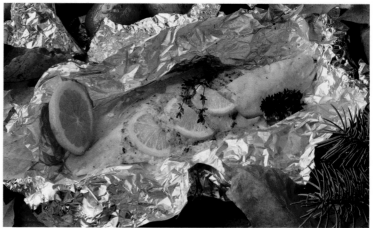

In-Fisherman PRESENTS Cooking FRESHWATER FISH

By Chef Lucia Watson

39

59

81

87

110

125

CELEBRATING OUR HARVEST

Selective Harvest and Concern for Keeping & Cooking the Catch

IN-FISHERMAN has always been about teaching anglers how to catch more fish, so they could enjoy themselves without perpetual frustration. Along the way over the past 30 years, we developed a sensible conservation ethic to accompany us in the field.

The fish we catch and keep to eat remain for most of us a critical part of fishing—a reward for our effort that goes beyond sport and ties us to the principle reason that most of our ancestors fished. For those ancestors, fish as food was usually more important than anything to do with sport. Today, in traditional fashion, most anglers still want to harvest at least some of their catch.

What has changed is that today, more and more anglers are harvesting fish selectively; that is, we let a portion of the catch go, particularly those large fish that usually are less abundant than smaller fish of the same species.

So, we release the eight-pound walleyes in favor of keeping several 16-inch fish, the makings of an exquisite meal. We also take home a mess of abundant panfish of a medium size—perch, bluegills, crappies, or white bass. This helps to sustain good fishing for larger fish, as we continue a tradition of eating the abundant fish, which also are nutritious and delicious.

In a sense, we harvest selectively as a matter of conscience and conservation concern. When fish are harvested wisely (selectively), they also are a renewable resource. We can continue to enjoy fine fishing today and continue to eat fish in the future.

« In-Fisherman Editor In Chief Doug Stange with a fish to be released.

Chef Lucia Watson

This ethic is the reason that, beginning in the 1980s, we began a column—Taste Tempters—about cooking the catch. As is true in the rest of *In-Fisherman* magazine, where foremost experts on fishing topics are the only ones qualified to address readers, so too would our Taste Tempters columnist have to be a topnotch professional working chef, the better if that columnist also understood fishing.

Lucia Watson—author, James Beard Award Nominee, and perennially popular Minneapolis, Minnesota, chef and owner of Lucia's Restaurant, has been that columnist since 1990.

Watson has distinguished herself, her restaurant, and *In-Fisherman* magazine quietly and consistently over the years with a steady insistence on exceptional quality in recipe writing, and in her reliance on the finest possible ingredients in her cooking, those ingredients changing with the seasons and with seasonal availability. Lucia is at her best cooking fresh fish.

Lucia's recipes and her cooking approaches always are as simple and easy to use as they are delicious. The longstanding popularity of her column is surely a result of her understanding that it isn't how well the teacher cooks, so much as how well the teacher gets the student to perform. This has been the collaboration between *In-Fisherman* and Chef Lucia for almost two decades.

Part of the essence of fishing is seeing the fish we catch reach the pan with a care borne of lives that have taught us how lucky we are to be able to partake of the bounty of this harvest.

—Doug Stange

Acknowledgements

WHILE I'M the author of this cookbook on behalf of *In-Fisherman*, it's really a collaboration by three of us, partners playing off each other's strengths.

Chuck Nelson, of Nelson Advertising Outfitters in Brainerd, Minnesota, is one of the finest food photographers in the business. He has been there to shoot every recipe of mine over the years, dating back to 1990. Once a recipe reaches the table, Chuck, with his superb eye for color combination

and layout proportion, always makes the necessary adjustments so that the final photo is perfect.

In-Fisherman Editor In Chief Doug Stange is the primary reason this book exists. He conceptualized the selective harvest ideal in the late 1980s and integrated it into every aspect of *In-Fisherman*. It was his idea to add a Taste Tempters column to the magazine, so that anglers could prepare their catch with the same panache they applied to catching them. He also authored the chapters on Cleaning the Catch and Keeping the Catch. And he has been the primary editor for all my writing, at times tempering my ideas so that anglers could understand them with ease. Thanks, Doug and Chuck, for always raving about my cooking.

Thank you, too, to other members of *In-Fisherman's* editorial team—from the Copy Editor Kathy Callaway and Editorial Assistant Claudette Kitzman, to the Production Assistants Amy Jackson and Jan Schneider, and Art Director Chuck Beasley. Jeff Simpson, meanwhile, is responsible for many of the field photos that accompany the Tips for each recipe, as well as for the photos that support Cleaning the Catch and Keeping the Catch.

Cooking has always been my passion, and I have been blessed to follow that path. My grandmother, Lulu, got me interested in cooking, Artie Lee taught me how to fish as a little girl, and my parents constantly encouraged me to pursue my dreams. Thank you, too, for the support offered by my brother Peter and my friend Beth Dooley. And my great, amazing staff at Lucia's, each of whom has helped to make the restaurant a success, assisted with details for some of the recipes in this book and continued my vision while I worked on it. Thanks to each of you.

—Lucia Watson

⌃ Lucia and Chuck Nelson prepping for a Taste Tempters photo shoot.

This Remarkable Bounty

FINE SPORT ASIDE, what's remarkable about even a modest catch of a half dozen nice perch is that they are the freshest fish on the face of the earth, the main ingredient for a meal fit for the richest person in the world.

If you read *In-Fisherman* magazine, you soon learn that there are no favorite fish species—and that's just as true in the catching as it is in the eating. Just as each species is unique in the challenges it presents in finding and catching, so does each species we decide to take home bring to the table its own unique qualities.

Walleye is, of course, wonderful—perhaps our most famous freshwater fish on the table. It's particularly mild, which is why it's such an all-around favorite with anglers. Fresh walleye does well with a light touch, a simple sautéeing after a light dusting in seasoned flour, the better if butter and some bacon grease enter the equation now and then.

Perch also do well prepared with an easy hand, while pike are more distinctive and are wonderful in a variety of recipes, from chowders to gratins to deep-fried. Indeed, pike is a favorite among many top anglers and guides who have eaten hundreds of meals of fish, whether prepared in shore-lunches, in restaurants, or in their own kitchens. They find it flavorful and nicely textured.

Small bass taste like large bluegills, which are in short supply in most waters; so we recommend keeping a small bass or two—usually plentiful—while releasing larger bluegills. We can find no better description for the taste of

bass and bluegills than "nut-like." It's a beautiful and distinctive flavor. They and crappies are delicate in their own way, delicious pan-fried and topped with a seasoned butter, as well as in many other recipes.

A cheer, too, for many more fish, from stream trout to lake trout, whitefish to catfish, sturgeon, white bass, and bullheads. Lucky also are those who can fish for salmon— coho, Kokanee, and kings.

And, for someone who revels in the differences in the taste of the various fish, this list could go on. Panfish are distinctively different when scaled and then filleted, instead of filleted with the skin removed; whereas larger fish tend to harbor ill-tasting fatty tissue just under the skin. In the final sections of this book we offer instruction in keeping the catch, as well as how to clean it appropriately for use in the recipes of this book.

As you know, there are so many different ways to prepare fish, so many different cooking approaches and recipes—and so many cookbooks. In this book, we offer a selection of recipes that are versatile, allowing easy substitution of one fish species for another, depending on just what you bring home. Saltwater fish species are easily adaptable here, as well. We also offer a primer in pairing wine that one can find and afford with fish recipes. Making appropriate selections isn't difficult.

One fundamental tenet of every recipe for the *In-Fisherman* Taste Tempters column is that it be superb on the table and yet easy to prepare . We don't want you wasting time or the fish you've caught.

Favorite
FISH CAKES

MANY PEOPLE PREFER fish cakes to any other way of preparing fish. The crunchy coating and moist interior make them a delicious main course—or shape them into smaller cakes and serve as an appetizer. This is perfect to make if you have leftover mashed potatoes.

To serve about six ...

Mashed Potatoes

1 lb. potatoes, mashed
2 tbsp. butter
1/2 c. cream
salt and pepper

» First, make perfect mashed potatoes. Peel the potatoes and cut them into equal chunks, place them in cold water with some salt, bring to a boil, lower heat, and cook until very tender. Drain and mash with the cream, butter, salt and pepper.

» Chill the mixture before proceeding.

Fish Cakes ...

1 lb. fish, bones removed
1 tbsp. lemon juice
pinch of cayenne
salt and pepper
1 tbsp. Worcestershire sauce
3 tbsp. minced scallion

a little cream
dried bread crumbs seasoned with salt and pepper
butter for sautéeing

» In small batches in a blender, purée the fish, adding the mashed potatoes, lemon juice, cayenne, salt and pepper, Worcestershire sauce, and minced scallions. The mixture should be thick and sticky. If it gets too thick, add more cream to loosen it and continue to purée.

» Test for final seasoning: Take a small spoonful of the mixture and form into a little "hamburger." Dust each side in flour. Sauté in butter over medium heat until browned. Flip and cook the other side. Taste, and adjust the seasoning if necessary.

» Shape into round cakes about 1/2 inch thick. Lightly dust with flour and sauté them in butter over medium heat.

» Serve with tartar sauce and lemon wedges.

Tartar Sauce ...

Combine:

1 c. mayonnaise; 2 tbsp. sweet pickles, chopped; 1 tbsp. capers, chopped; 1 tbsp. Dijon mustard; 1 tsp. fresh parsley, chopped; 1 tbsp. fresh tarragon, chopped (or 1 tsp. dry); 1 tsp. lemon juice; salt, pepper, and cayenne to taste.

» Combine all ingredients. Taste and add more lemon or salt and pepper if needed.

« FISH TIP: Redhorse suckers, which are fun to catch in spring and early summer, fight hard and have delicate flavor. Trim the dark, fatty strip along the outside of their fillets. Grinding gets rid of most of the small bones. Pick through the ground fish to remove any remaining large bones.

PAN-FRIED
Trout with Smoky Bacon, Hazelnuts, & Lemon Sage Butter

THIS RECIPE is reminiscent of summer canoe trips. We catch trout and fry them almost immediately over a campfire. The smoky bacon flavor with trout is a classic, and the nuts and herbs add crunch and depth. Serve with a wild rice pilaf. Simple and delicious!

To serve four . . .
    1 c. whole hazelnuts
    6 slices smoked country-style bacon
    4 trout (about 8 oz. each), cleaned and gutted
        with heads left on
    salt and freshly ground pepper
    8 scallions, washed and trimmed to length of fish
    flour seasoned with salt and freshly ground pepper
    1 stick (8 tbsp.) butter
    juice of 1 lemon
    12 large, fresh sage leaves

» Spread the hazelnuts on a baking sheet and toast in a preheated 350°F oven about 15 minutes, or until the skins split. Place them in a dish and cover with plastic wrap until they cool, then rub them with a towel to remove as much skin as possible. Chop the nuts.

» Cook the bacon in a large skillet until crisp, reserving the drippings in the skillet. Drain the bacon on paper towels.

» Salt and pepper the cavity of the trout. Dredge the trout in seasoned flour. Then place 2 trimmed scallions in the cavity of each fish.

» Heat the bacon drippings in the skillet and fry the trout, about 4 minutes per side.

» In a small saucepan, heat together the butter, lemon juice, and sage leaves. Spoon the lemon sage butter over the trout and sprinkle with the hazelnuts and crumbled bacon.

« FISH TIP: Small coho salmon and Kokanee salmon are exceptional in a recipe like this. Small lake trout work well, too. These cutthroat trout from an alpine lake in the Wind River Range, Wyoming, had brilliant orange flesh, a sign they had been feeding on tiny crustaceans.

» COOK'S TIP: You can adjust this recipe to suit any season by changing the nuts and the herbs: Use pecans and chives for a spring meal served with fresh steamed asparagus, and in summer, substitute basil and pine nuts and serve with sliced garden tomatoes. Such final visual and taste touches add appeal to any simple recipes.

Sautéed
WALLEYE
with Sour Cream and Dill

ACROSS MOST OF the North, walleye is the fish of choice with this recipe, as simple as it is sublime, but panfish like crappies, perch, or bluegill are good too—really, any delicate, white-fleshed fish.

To serve two . . .

2 fillets
1/4 c. flour
1/4 c. cornmeal
salt and pepper to taste
1 tbsp. unsalted butter
1 tbsp. olive oil

Sour Cream and Dill . . .

1/2 c. white wine
6 tbsp. sour cream
2 tbsp. fresh dill, chopped (2 tsp. dry)
1 tbsp. fresh parsley or chives, chopped
zest of 1 lemon, chopped

» Rinse the fillets and pat dry. Combine the flour, salt and pepper, and cornmeal, and dredge the fillets, shaking them lightly to remove excess flour.

» In a large skillet, heat the olive oil and butter until the foam subsides. Sauté the fillets over medium heat until golden, turning them once. Remove to two warm plates.

» Wipe any crumbs from the skillet and return to a medium-high flame. Add wine and cook for 5 to 8 minutes, or until the liquid is reduced by half. Whisk in the sour cream until smooth, remove from heat, and add herbs and lemon.

» Taste the sauce and season with salt and pepper. Pour the sauce over fish and serve immediately.

« **FISH TIP:** Because walleyes usually live in larger, clearer lakes, rivers, and reservoirs, they rarely absorb any "off" flavors associated with algae. Exceptions occur in late summer in some shallow lakes and reservoirs, but prime flavor returns to fish in these waters as algae dies. Fish consistently taste best taken from colder waters in winter, spring, and fall.

» **COOK'S TIP:** After cooking, keep prepared fish at or above 135°F or chill them below 41°F, as bacteria multiply rapidly between 41°F and 135°F. Fish that remain between 41°F and 135°F for more than a few hours should be discarded.

CATFISH
with Cajun Rub and Lime Cilantro Sour Cream

ONE OF MY favorite recipes for smaller catfish works well with any white-fleshed fish, from walleye to crappie. The lime cilantro sour cream (prepare this first) is distinctive, a cool contrast with the spicy fish. Serve with oven-roasted potatoes.

To serve four . . .

4 tsp. salt
2 tsp. cayenne (or to taste)
2 tsp. white pepper
4 tsp. dried thyme
2 tsp. dried basil
4 tsp. garlic powder
1 tbsp. paprika
1 c. flour
4 catfish fillets
2 tbsp. butter
2 tbsp. oil

» Combine all the herbs and spices. Add the flour and mix thoroughly.

» Lightly pat dry each catfish fillet with paper towels, then dredge each in the flour mixture, shaking off the excess.

» Melt the butter and oil in a large skillet until the butter foams.

» Fry the fillets over medium heat until golden brown (3 to 4 minutes), then flip and fry the other side.

» Place on a plate and top with Lime Cilantro Sour Cream.

Lime Cilantro Sour Cream . . .

Combine:
1/2 c. sour cream
4 tbsp. fresh cilantro, chopped
2 tbsp. fresh parsley, chopped
1 tbsp. fresh chives, finely minced
2 cloves garlic, finely minced
zest of 1 lime, finely chopped
juice of 1 lime
salt and pepper to taste
large dash Tabasco sauce

« FISH TIP: The clean, mild flavor of catfish lends itself wonderfully to a variety of cooking methods. The best size fillets for sautéeing range up to about 12 ounces. Bigger fillets are more difficult to cook evenly. Catfish with their denser flesh also take a little longer to cook than more delicate fish like walleye. Catfish also can stand a bit more heat.

» COOK'S TIP: While freshly caught and cleaned fish taste best, they also are difficult to sauté evenly because muscle rigor causes them to curl (or bulge in the middle) when they hit the pan. They actually cook best the day after the fact.

ALMOND
Crusted Walleye with Pears & Blue Cheese

I MAKE THIS WONDERFUL DISH in the late fall, when pears are in season and we crave richer, heartier foods. But of course it's nice during any season. I recommend accompanying this with a light green salad or blanched, crispy vegetables.

To serve two . . .

2 walleye fillets, about 1/2 lb. each
flour seasoned with salt and pepper
1 large egg, lightly beaten
3/4 c. sliced almonds
1 tbsp. butter
1 tbsp. oil
2 tbsp. minced scallion
1 ripe pear, cut into slices
1/4 c. white wine
1/4 c. heavy cream
salt and pepper to taste
juice of 1/2 lemon
2 tbsp. blue cheese, crumbled

» Dredge the fillets in the seasoned flour, shaking off any excess. Dip each fillet in egg and then press each side into the almonds.

» Melt the butter and oil until the foam subsides, then sauté the fillets about 5 or 6 minutes on each side or until tender. Transfer the fillets to a plate and cover to keep warm.

» Drain any excess grease from the pan. Add scallions and the pear slices and cook over medium heat 1 to 2 minutes. Add wine and cook a few more minutes, then add the cream and season with salt and pepper. Add the lemon juice and taste to adjust seasoning.

» At the last minute, add the crumbled blue cheese and spoon the mixture over each fillet.

« FISH TIP: Because blue cheese is so distinctive, it goes well with mild fish like walleye, but less well with more strongly flavored fish. So, this would also work with perch, bluegills, crappies (up to medium size) and smaller bass, but not so well with catfish, drum, white bass, or striper.

» COOK'S TIP: Blue cheeses vary enormously in flavor. For this dish, I like a milder domestic blue, like Maytag or Shepard's Way Big Woods Blue. When you sauté the fish, the heat should be medium so the almonds don't get too brown.

STIR-FRY
Catfish with Ginger & Sweet Peppers

CATFISH WORKS perfectly because it's so firm, but I often substitute walleye, bass, pike, or perch. Another firm and tasty fish is the burbot (eelpout)—and I use striped bass, when they're available. Rice always goes well with stir-fry.

To serve two or three . . .

1 tbsp. sesame oil
2 tbsp. soy sauce
1 tbsp. vegetable oil
1 lb. catfish fillets, cut into 1-inch cubes
1/2 red, yellow, and green bell peppers, cut into strips
1 carrot, cut into strips
1 tbsp. fresh ginger, grated
1 tbsp. fresh garlic, minced
2 scallions, coarsely chopped
1/4 c. fresh cilantro, steamed and chopped
toasted sesame seeds for garnish

» Blend the sesame oil and soy sauce and set aside. Heat the vegetable oil in a nonstick skillet until very hot.

» Add the fish, peppers, carrots, ginger, garlic, and scallions. Cook 3 to 5 minutes over high heat, stirring gently.

» Pour the sesame-soy mixture over the fish and cook one more minute. Turn off heat and gently stir in the cilantro. Serve with rice and sprinkle with sesame seeds.

« FISH TIP: Many saltwater fish are as flavorful and, often, even tastier than freshwater fish. The freshwater striper (rockfish or striped bass) is a saltwater transplant within the last century. Especially in smaller sizes, it's usually beautifully flavored and firmly textured, making it perfect in many recipes—especially stir-fries.

» COOK'S TIP: Keeping the heat high and stirring constantly are the keys to achieving crispy, brightly colored vegetables and a light, non-greasy product. Use a heavy sauté pan. Have all of the ingredients ready to go, get the oil very hot, shake the pan vigorously and often, and don't overcook.

STIR-FRY
Walleye with Sesame & Rice

ANOTHER EASY STIR-FRY that's appropriate any time of year, this dish is good for you—and tasty. I serve it over or alongside rice or noodles.

To serve four . . .

3 tbsp. dark sesame oil
1 lb. walleye fillets, cut into 1-inch cubes
1 tbsp. garlic, finely minced
1 tbsp. ginger, finely minced
3 to 4 c. mixed vegetables, cut into 2-inch chunks (carrot, celery, Napa cabbage or bok choy, cauliflower, broccoli, snow peas, sweet pepper)
1 tbsp. soy sauce, mixed with 4 tbsp. water
zest & juice of 1 lime or lemon
1 tbsp. fresh cilantro, chopped
cilantro sprigs for garnish
toasted sesame seeds for garnish

» In a heavy-bottomed skillet, heat the sesame oil over medium-high heat until hot. Add the fish and cook quickly, about 1 minute.

» Add the garlic, ginger, and all vegetables. Cook over high heat for 1 to 2 minutes, stirring and shaking the pan. Add the soy-water mixture all at once, stir, then cover the pan.

» Cook on high heat about 5 minutes. Taste the fish and vegetables to be sure they're cooked the way you like them, cooking longer if necessary. Vegetables should be crunchy and bright. Add the lime and chopped cilantro.

» Serve the stir-fry on rice or noodles, garnished with sesame seeds and cilantro sprigs.

« FISH TIP: This is a recipe in which a larger walleye works better than smaller pan-fry-sized fish. A larger fish is a little firmer and tends to hold together better in a stir-fry. Medium-sized pike like this one are another top stir-fry fish.

» COOK'S TIP: Walleye is so delicately textured that you must be careful stirring, or the fish falls apart. I use a larger spatula to gently turn the fish and the vegetables, and I shake the pan to move things around. I do my stir-frying with a sauté pan. A cast-iron pan works, too.

SESAME
Crusted Trout with Ginger Scallion Salad

I LOVE THE BRIGHTNESS and texture (the "crunch") of this dish any time of the year. In summer, serve this with a cool cucumber salad and in winter with some hot steamed jasmine rice.

To serve two . . .
- 1/2 c. lemon juice
- 4 tbsp. sesame seeds
- two 8- to 10-oz. fresh trout, butterflied
- salt and pepper
- 2 tbsp. butter
- 2 tbsp. dark sesame oil

» Dip each trout into the lemon juice. Season with salt and pepper and then dredge the skinless side in the sesame seeds to coat well.

» In a heavy-bottomed sauté pan, heat the butter and oil until the foam subsides. Place the trout sesame-side-down in the pan.

» Lower the heat to medium and cook about 5 to 8 minutes; flip, and cook another 5 to 8 minutes.

Ginger Scallion Salad...
- 1/4 c. fresh ginger thinly julienned, about 1 in. long
- 1/2 c. scallion thinly julienned, about 1 in. long
- 1 tbsp. soy sauce
- 1 tbsp. dark sesame oil
- 1 clove garlic, finely mashed
- pinch of sugar
- 1 tsp. red pepper flakes
- 1 tbsp. orange juice
- 1 tbsp. orange zest
- 1 tbsp. fresh mint, roughly chopped
- 1 tbsp. fresh cilantro, roughly chopped

» Combine all ingredients and taste for seasoning, adjusting if necessary. Pile a little of the salad on top of each trout.

《 FISH TIP: To keep the flesh firm and tight, don't rinse trout in water after you've butterflied them. Instead, rinse them thoroughly after you've gilled and gutted them, before butterflying. If you must freeze trout, try to use them as soon as possible. Better to cook all at once and make the extra into delicious Fish Mousse.

» **COOK'S TIP:** Smaller trout lend themselves to quick cooking as in the recipe above, while larger trout work better poached, baked, or broiled. Really big trout, 20 inches or more, are best stuffed and baked, or cut into fingers and deep-fried.

CRISPY FISH
with Asian Flavors

FOR MANY ANGLERS, there's nothing like the flavor and texture of a crisp, freshly fried fish. This recipe is easy and quick to prepare, and the dipping sauce—which can be prepared in advance—is a wonderful complement. Any white-fleshed fish works well, the fresher the better. I like this with steamed white rice or Japanese soba (buckwheat) noodles, tossed with soy sauce and cilantro.

To serve two...

fish of choice, small fillets cut into finger-sized strips,
    about 12 ounces total
1 c. cornmeal
1/2 c. flour
salt, pepper, dash of cayenne
oil in a deep, heavy pot, 3 to 4 inches deep (or, to sauté, oil
    in a heavy sauté pan)

» Combine the flour, cornmeal, salt, pepper, and cayenne.

» Lightly dust the fish fillets in the flour-and-cornmeal mixture, and fry in hot oil until just done and crispy. Drain on paper towels.

Dipping sauce...

6 tbsp. rice wine vinegar
3 tbsp. sugar
1 tbsp. dark soy sauce
1 jalapeño pepper, seeds removed, minced (or substitute a
    pinch of red pepper flakes)
2 tbsp. lime zest (grated lime peel)
juice of 1/2 lime
1 small knob ginger, peeled and grated fine
1 bud of garlic, peeled and finely minced
2 tbsp. fresh cilantro, chopped

» Boil the vinegar and sugar together until the sugar dissolves. Cool. Stir in the remaining ingredients. Taste and adjust the seasoning. This can be made well ahead of the fish.

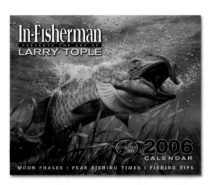

« FISH TIP: Many anglers believe that the positions of the sun and moon have a bearing on fishing, one reason In-Fisherman's annual calendars, which identify these Peak Fishing Periods, are so popular.

» COOK'S TIP: At the other end of the cooking spectrum, this dipping sauce goes well with poached or steamed fish.

BEER Batter Fish Fry

WHO DOESN'T LIKE the crunchy, rich flavor of deep-fried fish? In this recipe, the beer batter puts a light, crisp coating over the moist fish. Try it with any firm, white-fleshed fish. Freshly caught lake trout are nice, too. In the field, a coffee can over a campfire works fine (see Fundamental Shorelunch).

To serve four . . .

1½ lbs. firm white-fish fillets
3/4 c. flour
1 tsp. each salt and pepper
dash of cayenne pepper

The batter:
1/4 tsp. baking soda
1 c. milk
1 egg
2 tbsp. beer
6 c. oil for frying
2 tbsp. dark sesame oil (optional)

» Rinse the fillets, pat them dry, and cut them into finger shape, about 3 inches long and 1 inch wide. Keep them cold until ready to fry.

» Whisk together all the ingredients for the batter until smooth. Allow the batter to rest for about 15 minutes.

» Combine the flour with the salt, pepper, and cayenne. Lightly dust a fish finger in flour, immediately submerge it in the batter, shake off the excess, and lower it into the hot oil. Fry each batch 3 or 4 minutes until golden brown. Remove to a plate and let drain on paper towels.

» Serve this classic dish with tartar sauce along with fat wedges of lemon, or with malt vinegar.

» **COOK'S TIP:** A nice variation on this, especially for strongly flavored fish like white bass and sheepshead, is to marinate the fingers before deep-frying. Combine the marinade ingredients, pour over the fish portions, then let sit for an hour in the refrigerator. Drain off the marinade, pat the fish dry with a paper towel, dip in flour then batter, and deep-fry, as above. Substitute water or 7-Up instead of beer in the batter mix, as the taste of beer clashes with the marinade. This also is a fine marinade for grilling.

Tartar Sauce (makes about 1¾ c.) . . .

Whisk together:
1½ c. mayonnaise
1 dill pickle, minced
2 shallots, minced
1 tbsp. capers, chopped
1 tbsp. fresh parsley, chopped
1 tbsp. fresh chives, chopped
1 tbsp. Dijon mustard
salt and freshly ground pepper to taste
1 tsp. lemon juice
lemon wedges for garnish
malt vinegar

Orange Rum Marinade . . .

2 c. freshly squeezed orange juice; zest of 2 oranges; 2 tbsp. chopped mint; 2 tbsp. Grand Marnier liqueur; 1/2 c. Myers' Rum; 1/4 c. soy sauce; 1 tbsp. chopped garlic.

» COOK'S TIP: Cut the fish into consistent pieces so they fry evenly. Be sure the oil's hot—between 360°F and 380°F. A little dark sesame-seed oil added to the peanut or corn oil adds a nice nutty flavor. Fry the fish in a deep pan four or five pieces at a time, allowing the oil to reheat between batches. This batter also works for shrimp and vegetables.

PANFISH Tempura

SMALL CRAPPIES and, particularly, bluegills are my favorite tempura fish, although many people prefer perch. Any panfish will do—as will finger-sized strips cut from the fillets of larger fish. Serve with a dipping sauce like the one I offer here, or with one of our Marinades.

For the tempura (serves four) . . .

12 small panfish fillets, patted dry
Assorted fresh, seasonal vegetables of your choice cut into large pieces—green & red bell peppers, asparagus, mushrooms, red onions, snow peas, sweet potatoes

For the batter . . .

2 eggs
2 c. sifted all-purpose flour
2 c. ice-cold beer (or water)
extra flour for dipping, mixed with salt & pepper

» Set up the ingredients in the frying area in assembly-line fashion: (1) prepared fish and vegetables, (2) flour for dipping, (3) batter, (4) fryer with oil, and (5) pan lined with paper towels to drain finished tempura.

» To make the batter, beat the eggs slightly, then add ice-cold beer (or water) and mix lightly. Add the flour and beat a few times with a fork or until the ingredients are loosely combined. The batter should be lumpy. Heat the oil to 360°F.

» Dip the fish and vegetables in flour, shake off the excess, and dip them in the batter. Slide the pieces into hot oil and fry until golden—about 3 to 4 minutes. Drain on paper towels and serve at once with dipping sauce.

Ginger Dipping Sauce . . .

5 tbsp. water
1 tbsp. ginger, finely grated
1 tbsp. garlic, finely minced
1 tbsp. dark sesame oil
5 tbsp. soy sauce
2 tbsp. scallion, finely minced
2 tbsp. fresh cilantro, chopped
2 tbsp. lime, lemon, or orange juice
2 tbsp. fresh mint, chopped
pinch of red chili flakes

» Combine the ingredients and stir well.

« FISH TIP: Bluegills are one of the most distinctive-tasting freshwater fish of all, with a sweet, nutty flavor. Smaller largemouth bass taste somewhat similar—wonderful, too. Rock bass (goggle-eyes) also are excellent.

» COOK'S TIP: The key to tempura is that the ingredients must be fresh and cold. Cut the vegetables into even-sized pieces and adjust cooking time for each. For example, a sweet potato must cook longer than a green pepper. Be sure the oil is at a constant minimum of 360°F—and not much hotter. The batter should be lumpy and never mixed too well.

DEEP-FRIED
(or Sautéed) Catfish with Chili Cornmeal Crust, and Sweet Pepper, Corn, & Bacon Relish

THE SWEET PEPPER, corn, and bacon relish is a classic with any fried fish, particularly during summer when corn and peppers are ripe and super-sweet.

To serve two . . .

1/2 c. cornmeal
1/2 c. flour
1/4 tsp. chili powder
salt and pepper
1/2 c. fresh lemon juice
2 fillets, about 8 oz. each, rinsed in cold water and patted dry
2 tbsp. vegetable oil or bacon fat, or an inch of oil in a deeper pan for deep-frying

» Combine the cornmeal, flour, chili powder, salt and pepper. Dip each fillet in lemon juice then in the cornmeal mixture, carefully dusting each side of the fillets.

» Heat the fat in a heavy-bottomed skillet until it just starts to smoke. Put the fillets in the fat and cook about 5 minutes until golden brown.

» Turn the fillets and continue to cook about 4 minutes on the other side. If deep-frying, cook the fillets without turning, about 7 to 8 minutes or until golden brown.

» Remove the fish to a plate and garnish with the warm sweet relish or the horseradish sauce.

Sweet Pepper, Corn, & Bacon Relish...

3 slices bacon, finely diced
1/2 each green, red, and yellow bell peppers, seeded and diced, about 2 c. total
1 small red onion, diced
2 ears fresh corn (slice kernels off cobs), about 2 c.
1 tbsp. fresh thyme
1 tbsp. fresh chives
salt and pepper to taste

» Place the bacon in a heavy-bottomed saucepan. Cook until the fat starts to render and the bacon gets crispy.

» Immediately add the peppers, onion, and corn. Cook over high heat stirring constantly, until the veggies are crispy and warmed through.

» Add the herbs and taste for final seasoning.

Horseradish Sour Cream Sauce...

Another simple sauce for any sautéed or deep-fried fish.

Mix together:

1 c. sour cream
2 heaping tbsp. prepared horseradish
juice of 1/2 lemon
salt and pepper
1 tbsp. fresh chives or parsley, chopped

« **FISH TIP:** The perfect ending to a summer day of wading a small river for channel catfish: A few smaller catfish have been harvested for a fine meal.

» **COOK'S TIP:** In colder months, when we can't get fresh sweetcorn, this Horseradish Sour Cream Sauce is a good complement to fried catfish. It also makes a fine dipping sauce for the Beer Batter Fish Fry. And it's good with potatoes, baked or deep-fried.

BEER BATTER
Fingers with Maple-Mustard Dipping Sauce

THIS IS ANOTHER distinctive recipe for beer-batter fish. The batter here is just a little bit different, an alternative to thinner mixes. Meanwhile, the simple maple-mustard dipping sauce is one of my all-time favorites. I use walleye to do this recipe, but any lean fish works just as well. Perhaps my overall favorite is perch.

To serve one or two . . .
    1/2 c. flour
    salt and pepper to taste
    1/4 tsp. baking powder
    1/4 tsp. dry mustard
    1/2 tsp. cayenne powder
    1/2 c. beer (room temperature)
    oil for deep frying
    2 walleye fillets, bones removed,
        cut into fingers or appropriate portions

» Combine the flour, salt, pepper, baking powder, mustard, and cayenne in a bowl. Add the beer and whisk. (If you use cold beer, let the batter sit for an hour after mixing.)

» In a heavy pot, heat the oil to 350°F. Test the oil by sprinkling a few drops of batter into it. The batter droplets should sizzle and immediately rise to the top of the oil.

» Dip the fish in the batter and thoroughly coat each fillet. Fry until crisp and golden, about 3 to 5 minutes. Remove with a slotted spoon and drain on paper towels.

Maple-Mustard Dipping Sauce...
    1/2 c. smooth Dijon mustard
    3 tbsp. maple syrup

» Mix together and taste for seasoning.

« FISH TIP: If yellow perch aren't the finest-tasting freshwater fish of all, they at least rank near the top in any voting. The flesh is firm and mild. For deep-frying, I cut large fillets into three portions. Small fillets can be fried whole.

» SERVING TIP: Deep-fried fish strips like these also dress up nicely served in a basket or on a plate with fresh fruit, like grapes and strawberries.

Steamed
SALMON STEAKS
with Chardonnay Butter Sauce

WHAT BETTER WAY than to celebrate the year's ending and a new beginning with a beautiful salmon steak covered in a rich butter sauce. The fish can be either baked or steamed.

To serve four . . .

cut-up carrot, celery, and onion, about 1 c. each to enhance the flavors
a few sprigs fresh tarragon, parsley or dill
About 1 gallon water, depending on size of pot. The water should not touch the fish.
5 oz. salmon steak per serving

» To steam the steaks: In a heavy pot with a steaming platform and a tight lid, bring the water, vegetables, and herbs to a boil.

» Lower the fish onto the rack and steam on high for 5 to 7 minutes.

» Place the fish on a serving plate, spoon the sauce over the steaks and garnish with lemon or chopped fresh parsley.

» Or, to bake the steaks: Lightly oil a baking dish and add the steaks, surrounding them with the vegetables.

» Sprinkle the herbs over everything. Add a splash of white wine here and there, then bake for about 8 to 10 minutes at 400°F.

Chardonnay butter sauce . . .

1 c. Chardonnay wine
1 c. white wine vinegar
1/3 c. chopped shallots
1/8 inch of vanilla bean (at most)
salt and white pepper
8 oz. butter

» Bring the ingredients except the butter to a boil and reduce to 2 1/2 tablespoons. Strain, and return the reduced mixture to a heavy pot. Over low heat, slowly whisk in 8 ounces of cold butter one ounce at a time, whisking constantly until the mixture is smooth and emulsified. Season with salt and pepper.

« FISH TIP: With salmon, the fat content of the flesh is considered the indicator of table quality and flavor, much as with beefsteak—with higher fat content being better. With fish, fat content is related to how far the fish have to swim in their annual breeding cycle. Alaskan Copper River salmon are one of the most famous and delicious salmon, because the Copper River with its tributaries is one of the longest river systems in Alaska.

» COOK'S TIP: Steaming requires thorough and immediate immersion into hot mist. Begin with the pot full of steam. The steaming vessel needs to be high and wide so that steam can circulate around the food.
Since food doesn't contact any other medium when steamed, flavors are accentuated; therefore, using fish of fine quality is important. Keep cooking times as short as possible. Don't cook the soul out of the fish.

Baked
WALLEYE
with Red Wine Butter Sauce

A RICH, BUTTERY SAUCE looks beautiful on a baked white walleye fillet, or any other whitefish. The color contrast makes a lovely presentation.

To serve four . . .

4 walleye fillets, 6 to 8 oz. each
1 c. water
juice of 1/2 lemon
4 tbsp. butter, cut into pieces
salt and pepper to taste

The fish . . .

» Place fillets in an oven-safe glass dish. Add water and lemon juice to just cover the bottom of the dish.

» Heat oven to 375°F. Dot the fish with the butter, season with salt and pepper, and bake for about 8 minutes, or until the fish is just cooked.

» Remove the fish to plates and serve with the red-wine shallot sauce.

The sauce . . .

2 shallots, minced
1¾ c. red wine
1/4 c. fine-quality red wine vinegar
8 oz. very cold butter, cut into pieces
salt and pepper

» Combine the shallots, the wine, the vinegar, and a touch of salt and pepper and bring the mixture to a boil over moderate heat. Reduce this to 3 tablespoons—about 20 minutes.

» Remove from the heat and whisk in 2 tablespoons of butter. Then return to heat and whisk in 2 more tablespoons of butter. Slowly whisk in the remaining butter, 1 tablespoon at a time, over low heat, whisking constantly.

» Remove from the heat and adjust the seasoning. Spoon over the fish and garnish with chopped parsley.

» **FISH TIP:** Commercial walleye and catfish usually are, at a minimum, several days old when we buy them. I make sure it's been well cared for and it's always good—but never so fresh as fish we catch and clean ourselves. Still, if you try to cook this on the day you catch and clean the fish, the fillets will curl because of muscle rigor. Store the fillets in the refrigerator for a day before making this recipe.

» **COOK'S TIP:** For smaller panfish fillets such as perch or crappies, use two fillets for each serving. Lay one fillet flat, then lay another fillet on top of that fillet upside down, nestling the loin of one in the rib cavity of the other.

Fish Baked in an
HERB CRUST

THIS IS a nice presentation for any firm-textured, dense fish, from catfish to sturgeon, striper, or salmon, in steak or fillet. Try it with steamed new potatoes tossed in lemon and parsley butter, along with a medley of fresh vegetables.

To serve six . . .

6 fish steaks or fillets (about 1 inch thick)
1/2 c. chopped onion
1 c. chopped fresh herbs (try parsley, thyme, tarragon, and chervil)
1/2 c. breadcrumbs
1 stick (8 tbsp.) soft butter
1/4 c. fresh lemon juice
salt and freshly ground pepper to taste
white wine (or water)

» Rinse the fish portions and pat dry.

» In a food processor fitted with a steel blade, mix together all the ingredients except the wine and fish. Taste the mixture and adjust the seasoning.

» Pat equal amounts of this herb blend on top of each fish portion, then place them on a buttered rack set over a pan.

» Fill the bottom of the pan with about 1 inch of white wine or water. Bake the fish in a preheated 350°F oven for about 15 to 20 minutes or until the flesh flakes.

« FISH TIP: Most of the recipes in this book work perfectly with many saltwater fish. This is a favorite for redfish, a popular inshore species.

» **COOK'S TIP:** A simple and delicious vegetable medley for fall and winter: Choose at least three vegetables—carrots, cabbage, leeks, parsnips, rutabagas, or turnips. Cut them into thin strips and sauté in a bit of olive oil—or steam them. Add butter and a little chopped scallion.

Creole
CASSEROLE

A ZESTY WINTER DISH that's similar to the shrimp etoufée of Louisiana fame, a casserole that's distinctively flavored, so it's nice with fish that have been frozen. Any firm white-fleshed fish works—catfish, particularly well.

To serve four . . .

3 tbsp. butter or vegetable oil
5 tbsp. flour
1 med. onion, diced
2 garlic cloves, finely diced
1 green pepper, diced
2 celery stalks, diced
1 or 2 tbsp. Creole seasoning (recipe follows)
2 c. chicken or fish stock
1 tbsp. tomato purée (or paste)
4 catfish or walleye fillets, 6 to 8 ounces each,
   bones removed and fillets cut into 1-inch chunks

» In a pot over medium-low heat, melt the butter and whisk in the flour, stirring until the roux turns the color of a brown paper bag (perhaps 10 minutes but more typically 30 minutes or longer). Add the vegetables and one or two tablespoons of the Creole seasoning and cook for about five minutes, stirring often.

» To the simmering mixture, add the chicken stock and the tomato purée, stir, then simmer lightly for 10 minutes. Add more Creole seasoning to taste. At this point, the mixture can be chilled for later use.

» Place the fish chunks into a lightly oiled casserole dish, add the Creole mix, and bake covered at 350°F for 15 to 20 minutes—until just hot and bubbly. Serve over rice. Garnish with scallions.

Creole Seasoning . . .

Combine:
1 tbsp. salt
1 tbsp. cayenne
1 tbsp. white pepper
1 tbsp. dried basil
1 tbsp. black pepper
1 tsp. dried thyme

« FISH TIP: Of the three primary catfish species—channel, blue, and flathead—the flathead (pictured) is by far the finest eating. Indeed, it's one of the finest-tasting freshwater fish—true, surprisingly, even when they are large. Channel cats over 10 pounds often aren't so good to eat, although they work in a recipe like this. Blue cats often grow fast and may still be quite young, tender, and tasty in larger size-classes. The best-tasting usually weigh less than about 15 pounds. Trim portions of fillets to a size appropriate to this recipe.

» COOK'S TIP: My first cookbook, *Savoring the Seasons of the Northern Heartland*, co-authored with Beth Dooley (Alfred A. Knopf, Inc.), offers 200 seasonal recipes on cooking and harvesting traditions in the North Country. It's also available in paperback from the University of Minnesota Press.

Holiday
TROUT

TURKEY, HAM, or goose is the traditional focus of most holiday menus, but why not fish, for a change of pace? A whole stuffed trout makes a dramatic presentation and a delicious celebration. Present the fish at the table on a big platter surrounded by the extra stuffing, then salute the season with a hearty toast. Brook trout or lake trout are favorites, but other trout, including small steelhead, are good, too.

To serve four . . .

1 c. wild rice
4 slices bacon, diced
1 celery rib, diced
1 carrot, diced
1 med. onion, diced
1 orange peel, chopped
1 tsp. dried thyme
1/2 tsp. dried sage
1/2 c. currants or raisins
1 c. orange juice
1/2 c. heavy cream
1 c. white wine
1 trout or salmon, about 4 lbs.
1/4 c. butter
salt and pepper to taste

» Gut, scale, and split the fish down the backbone; pat dry; rub inside and out with butter, and season with salt and pepper. (The fish can also be butterflied, but I leave the head on for fancy table presentations.)

» For the stuffing, soak 1/2 cup of currants or raisins in 1 cup of orange juice. Meanwhile, cook 1 cup of wild rice in 3 cups of water with salt and pepper, until the rice pops and becomes tender. Drain the water and add the currants and orange juice, along with 1/2 cup of heavy cream.

» Over medium heat, sauté the diced bacon until crisp. Add the diced onion, carrot, celery, and orange peel, plus the sage and thyme. Cook until the onion is translucent, about 3 to 5 minutes. Transfer to a bowl and stir in the wild-rice mixture; taste and adjust the seasoning as needed.

» Stuff the cavity of the trout. (If the fish is butterflied, arrange the stuffing on one side of the fish and lay the other side over the stuffing.) Place the fish on aluminum foil and fold up the sides, leaving the top of the fish exposed. Pour the wine over the fish, dot with butter, and bake at 350°F for 45 minutes to 1 hour. Heat the remaining stuffing in a casserole dish.

« COOK'S TIP: This recipe works with a whole gutted trout or make it with fillets, baked or sautéed, and lay them on top of the oven-warmed stuffing. Another option is to butterfly the trout and stuff the two connected fillets.

WALLEYE

with Vegetables & Herbed Butter in Parchment

THE FRENCH call this method of cooking en papillote. The food is wrapped in parchment paper (or foil), baked in an oven then opened at the table, where the sudden burst of aromatic steam is wonderful. This easy, informal dinner entrée is healthful, as well.

I often prepare the parchment packages at noon and keep them refrigerated until about an hour before guests arrive for the evening meal. Remove the packages from the refrigerator at least half an hour before cooking.

Ingredients per person . . .

1 walleye fillet (or catfish, striped bass, or several panfish)
1 small pat of butter
salt and pepper to taste
1 tbsp. minced fresh herbs
splash of white wine
assorted colorful cut vegetables—your choice

» Cut one large square of parchment paper or foil into a heart shape. Spread one side thinly but completely with butter.

» Place the fillet on the butter and sprinkle with salt and pepper. Place the vegetables on top and around the fillet. Sprinkle with the wine and herbs.

» Fold the parchment paper or foil in half over the walleye. Overlap the edges, holding down creased edges with one index finger, using the other thumb and index finger to pinch and fold. Tuck the excess under and place on a baking sheet.

» Bake 12 to 15 minutes at 425°F. Serve immediately.

« FISH TIP: The sauger is closely related to walleye but generally doesn't get as large. It tastes similar to walleye, too (delicious!), and goes well in any of our recipes that call for walleye or another white-fleshed fish.

» COOK'S TIP: This is a nice way to prepare and present small, whole fish, such as panfish or white bass. Leave the head on and don't forget to eat the cheeks. Be sure to cut the vegetables into small pieces so they cook the same amount of time as the fish. If you use longer-cooking vegetables, such as potatoes or carrots, blanch them first, let them cool, then wrap with the fish.

Irish
FISH PIE

ESPECIALLY INVITING after a chilly day of fishing on ice or open water, I make this hearty dish using whatever I've caught—usually walleye or crappie. Friends have also used burbot (eelpout), lake trout, and pike. Catfish would be excellent.

To serve six . . .

2 tbsp. butter
1 med. onion, peeled and diced
3 small carrots, diced
2¼ c. mushrooms, washed and sliced
2 tbsp. flour
2½ c. milk
splash of sherry or white wine
salt and pepper
1/2 tsp. dried thyme (or 1 tbsp. fresh, chopped)
dash of cayenne
1 small bay leaf
splash of cream
2 lbs. filleted fish, deboned and cut into 2-inch pieces
2 tbsp. fresh parsley, chopped
3 cups of mashed potatoes, or about 1 cup of seasoned bread crumbs mixed with 1/2 cup grated Parmesan cheese

» Melt 2 tablespoons of butter in a heavy sauté pan. Add the onion, carrots, and mushrooms and sauté over medium heat, stirring occasionally until juicy and tender, about 10 minutes.

» Sprinkle the flour over the vegetables and stir. Cook a few more minutes.

» Add the milk, white wine, salt, pepper, thyme, cayenne, bay leaf, and a splash of cream. Cook over medium heat, stirring frequently until the mixture begins to thicken.

» Add the fish and parsley. Cook 5 minutes or until fish is just barely done. Taste and adjust the seasoning.

» Spoon into one large buttered ovenproof dish or six small ones. The recipe can be prepared ahead of time, up to this point.

» Spoon the mashed potatoes decoratively over the pie, or sprinkle with breadcrumbs and Parmesan. Drizzle with extra butter if desired.

» Bake at 350°F to brown the potato crust, about 15 minutes if the filling and potatoes are warm or 30 minutes if cold.

« FISH TIP: The color of pike flesh—generally white, though not so pearly white as walleye—varies, based on what the fish are eating. In waters with smelt and ciscoes, pike flesh often becomes decidedly reddish to yellow-orange, almost as colorful as trout flesh—especially in winter. These fish taste wonderful.

» COOK'S TIP: Fish Pie is close to being a complete meal. I add a simple green salad and a glass of red wine like a pinot noir, which goes well with most dishes that contain quite a few mushrooms. A dry riesling would be another fine choice—or a Guinness beer, to keep things Irish.

WALLEYE
in a Mustard Caraway Crust

TRY THIS DELICIOUS RECIPE for frozen fish, as the distinctive coating can cover any freezer flavors. It also works well with stronger-tasting fish like sheepshead and large white bass. Whether the fish are fresh or frozen, it's a nice detour from more typical preparations.

To serve four...

1 tbsp. caraway seeds, finely crushed
1/4 c. Dijon mustard
black pepper to taste
1 tbsp. butter
4 walleye fillets, 6 to 8 oz. each, bones removed
1 c. fresh rye breadcrumbs
2 tbsp. fresh parsley, chopped

» Preheat the oven to 425°F. Combine the caraway, mustard, and pepper. Butter a heavy baking dish.

» Lay out the fillets and coat with the mustard mixture. Pat on the rye breadcrumbs. Bake until cooked through—about 8 to 10 minutes.

» Arrange the individual servings on plates and sprinkle with parsley. Serve the fish with a colorful coleslaw.

« FISH TIP: Sheepshead (freshwater drum) are one of those common fish that can, with a little care and recipe tempering (as is the case here), be fine tablefare. Be sure to trim the red lateral line flesh from the outside of a fillet. Use only the best part of a fillet, discarding belly and rib meat.

» COOK'S TIP: When menu planning, side dishes are a wonderful way to make a plate attractive and healthy. Always think what's in season or what flavors bring out the best in the chosen entrée. The mustard and caraway here go well with an easy, crunchy coleslaw (see recipe in this book). Keep it simple, keep it seasonal: lightly blanched asparagus in spring. Sliced ripe tomatoes with chopped basil and an ear of sweetcorn for summertime. In the autumn, a baked squash with wild rice and, during winter months, braised white beans with a bit of bacon and some blanched carrots.

One handy kitchen rule: If the entrée is even slightly complicated, accompany it simply.

Grilled
CATFISH
with Sweetcorn Sauce

MAKE THIS DISH in the heat of summer when the corn is super sweet. Serve with sliced heirloom tomatoes drizzled with olive oil, balsamic vinegar, and snipped fresh chives.

To serve four . . .

4 catfish fillets, about 8 oz. each

The sauce . . .

2 tbsp. butter
1 small onion, diced
2 c. fresh sweetcorn, shucked
dash of white wine
2 c. cream
salt and pepper
1 tbsp. fresh parsley, chopped
1 red bell pepper, finely diced (about 1 c.)
whole tomatoes, sliced (heirloom tomatoes, if avail.)
1 tbsp. fresh chives, chopped
olive oil
balsamic vinegar

» Melt the butter in a heavy saucepan, add the onion and corn, cook over medium heat about 5 minutes, stirring occasionally.

» Add the white wine, cream, and salt and pepper. Bring to a boil, then immediately remove from the heat. Place half the mixture in a blender. Pulse-blend until just chunky and combine with the remaining cream mixture.

» Return to the heat and add the parsley and red bell pepper. Keep warm.

» Grill the fish over medium coals; place the fillets on plates, then spoon on the sauce.

« COOK'S TIP: Catfish works well on the grill because it stays firm and keeps its shape over the coals. For more delicate fish such as walleye, and for small panfish like crappies, it's best to use a grill basket.

» COOK'S TIP: Here's a **Sweetcorn Relish** that goes well with grilled, baked, or sautéed fish anytime of the year (makes about 1½ quarts): 12 ears of fresh corn; 12 ripe tomatoes, peeled, seeded & diced; 2 tbsp. salt; 2 green & 2 red bell peppers, diced same size as corn; 1/2 tsp. pepper; 1 c. cider vinegar; 1/2 c. water; 1 cucumber, diced same size as corn; 1/2 tsp. turmeric; 1 c. sugar; 1½ tsp. mustard seed. Shuck the corn off the cob. Mix all ingredients together in a pot, cover, and simmer for 45 minutes. Seal the relish in a jar and keep in the refrigerator.

Chili-Dusted
CATFISH
with Cumin Rice

THIS PERFECTLY simple recipe never fails to get rave reviews. A dollop of sour cream sprinkled with chili or paprika, plus a little parsley, is the perfect garnish. You'll be tempted to serve it often.

To serve two . . .

2 tsp. paprika
1 tsp. chili powder
2 tsp. salt
1/2 tsp. cayenne
1/4 c. buttermilk (or whole milk)
1 egg
pinch of sugar
2 catfish fillets
1/2 c. dry bread crumbs

» Preheat the oven to 400°F. Lightly grease a cookie sheet. Mix together the spices.

» In a shallow bowl, beat together the buttermilk, eggs, and sugar.

» One at a time, dip each fillet in the spice mix, then the buttermilk mixture, and finally the breadcrumbs. Place each fillet on the greased cookie sheet. Bake the fish until cooked through, about 12 to 14 minutes. Serve with the cumin rice.

Cumin Rice . . .

1 tbsp. butter
1 tbsp. minced garlic
1 tsp. ground cumin
1/2 tsp. dried oregano
1 c. long grain rice
2 c. chicken stock or water
1 tsp. salt
1/2 tsp. pepper
1/4 c. minced scallion
1 tsp. additional butter

» In a large, heavy-bottomed saucepan, heat the butter until melted. Add the garlic, cumin, oregano, and the rice. Cook, stirring about 3 minutes.

» Add the stock, salt, and pepper. Bring to a boil, reduce heat and cook covered for about 15 minutes, or until the liquid is absorbed and the rice is tender.

» Turn off the rice and allow it to sit, covered, for about 5 minutes. Stir in the additional butter and scallions and fluff with a fork.

« FISH TIP: This recipe is delicious with large crappie fillets, but harvest these fish very selectively.

» **COOK'S TIP:** For a variation on the rice, dice equal amounts of onion, carrot, and celery (about 1/2 cup each) and sauté in butter over medium heat for several minutes or until soft and translucent. Add a pinch of saffron or turmeric. Add cooked rice (about 4 cups to serve four) and stir to combine. Before serving, add more butter, along with about 1/4 cup each of chopped parsley and scallions. Season with salt and pepper.

WALLEYE
and Potato Au Gratin

SIMPLE, HEARTY, delicious: I often make this casserole the day before an ice-fishing excursion and store it overnight in the refrigerator. It's easy to pop into the oven for dinner after a day of chilly weather. I love this served with a light green salad, crunchy bread, and a glass of red wine. It works well with other white-fleshed fish and should be fine with lean lake trout.

To serve four ...

3 lg. baked potatoes, cooled
1/4 c. green onions, chopped
2 c. filleted and deboned fish, cut into 1-inch cubes
3/4 c. sharp cheddar cheese, grated
2 c. sour cream
salt and pepper to taste
dash of Tabasco sauce
sprinkle of paprika

» Peel the baked potatoes and cut them into cubes the same size as the fish portions.

» Combine all ingredients except the paprika in a greased casserole dish. Cover and refrigerate at least 3 hours or overnight, so the flavors mix.

» Sprinkle the top with paprika and bake at 350°F for 30 to 45 minutes, until hot and bubbly.

« FISH TIP: Lake trout are a fatty fish compared to white-fleshed fish like the walleye. Big lake trout such as those from the Great Lakes, having grown older and larger feeding on fatty prey like alewives, are difficult to use in most recipes because of their fat content. By comparison, smaller lake trout from the infertile waters of Canada and other parts of the U.S. are leaner and sometimes more adaptable to recipes for leaner fish.

» COOK'S TIP: A variety of gratin dishes allows for larger servings and different table presentations. You can make this dish seasonal by adding simple ingredients: In summer add 1 cup freshly shucked raw sweetcorn. In autumn, add 1/2 cup cooked wild rice; in winter, add 1 cup sautéed, sliced mushrooms. And in spring, add 1 cup of 1-inch pieces of fresh asparagus.

Baked
CATFISH
with Jalapeño, Tomato & Garlic, Guacamole, and Refried Black Beans

A MODESTLY SPICY little number like this one is a favorite with anyone who likes Mexican flavors. Because of the hearty flavors, this is a good recipe for frozen fish.

To serve two . . .

1 Roma tomato, diced
1/4 onion, minced
2 jalapeño chili peppers, cut into rounds (substitute red and yellow bell peppers for a less fiery taste)
2 tbsp. fresh cilantro, minced
salt and pepper to taste
2 tbsp. olive oil
2 tbsp. lime juice
2 garlic cloves, mashed
1 tbsp. tequila (optional)
salt to taste
two 6- to 8-ounce catfish fillets

» Combine all of the ingredients except the catfish fillets.

» Place the fillets on a lightly greased baking sheet and spoon the tomato-chili mixture over each. Bake at 350°F for about 15 minutes or until the flesh is opaque and flaky.

» Serve with refried black beans and guacamole.

Refried Black Beans . . .

1 tbsp. bacon fat or olive oil
1/2 onion, minced
2 cloves garlic, mashed
2 c. or one can cooked black beans
1/2 tsp. ground cumin
1/2 tsp. ground chili powder
1 tsp. salt

» Heat the olive oil or bacon fat in a skillet. Add the onion and garlic; cook until translucent over medium heat, about 5 minutes.

» Add the beans and cook, mashing the beans against the skillet with a fork or spatula so they become mushy, with most of the liquid cooked out (add a little water if they seem too dry).

» Add the seasonings and adjust to taste.

My Favorite Guacamole . . .

« Mash all ingredients together: 2 ripe avocados, peeled and pitted and diced; 2 cloves garlic, mashed; juice of 1 lime; small tomato, finely minced; 1/2 onion, finely minced; few drops olive oil; a pinch each of salt and pepper.

» COOK'S TIP: To remove odor from cooking utensils, hands, or fillet knives, rub them with a mixture of salt and lemon juice or vinegar.

WALLEYE

Baked with Hazelnuts and Sage

I'VE ALWAYS USED WALLEYE in this recipe, but most fish should be fine, including lake trout—even smaller whole stream trout, perhaps butterflied. During fall and winter, this goes well with wild rice and baked acorn squash. In spring, I substitute cumin rice (see Chili-Dusted Catfish) for the wild rice, and add a light green salad. Pecans substitute nicely for hazelnuts.

To serve two . . .

Cook first:
1 c. wild rice
1 acorn squash

Then:
2 fresh walleye fillets
2 tbsp. butter, plus a little more to grease the cookie sheet
2 tbsp. fresh sage, chopped
1 tbsp. hazelnuts, toasted and lightly chopped
salt and pepper
fresh lemon squeeze
1 tbsp. hazelnuts, toasted and lightly chopped

» Heat the oven to 375°F. Rinse the fish in ice-cold water and pat dry with paper towels.

» Lightly grease a cookie sheet with butter. Lay the fish on the cookie sheet and sprinkle with salt and pepper. Bake the fish about 8-12 minutes or until the flesh is opaque and tender.

» While the fish is baking, melt the butter. Just before the fish is done, add the sage to the butter, and a squeeze of fresh lemon juice.

» Spoon the butter and sage mixture over the fish and sprinkle hazelnuts on top.

Wild Rice . . .

» Measure the rice into a strainer and rinse. Put 3 to 4 cups of water in a saucepan and bring to a boil. Add the rice and a pinch of salt, and cover. Return the water to a boil, then reduce the heat to a simmer and cook for about 50 minutes or until the rice puffs open. Strain the water. Toss with salt, pepper, and butter to taste.

Acorn Squash . . .

» Heat the oven to 350°F. Cut the squash in half and scoop out the seeds. Put the squash into a baking pan with about a half inch of water. Sprinkle the squash with salt, brown sugar, and a tablespoon of butter. Cover lightly with foil and bake for about 45 minutes, or until the flesh is soft.

« **FISH TIP:** Even giant old alligator gar are edible, although we're on a mission to convince more people to let them go to sustain good fishing. The loin portion of gar can be cut into fingers and deep-fried; ground and made into "gar balls" or cakes; or sliced thinly and baked, as in this recipe.

WALLEYE
with Mushroom Cream Sauce and Wild Rice

MY GUESS IS THAT THIS will be one of your most popular recipes, really so good that you'll want to serve it to everyone. It works just as well with other fish, such as small largemouth bass or crappies, perch, bluegills, and pike.

To serve two . . .

2 tbsp. butter
1 c. mixed mushrooms, chopped—button, shitake, and wild varieties
1 leek, sliced into rounds 1/4 inch thick, then halved (or 1/2 c. chopped scallion)
1/4 c. dry sherry
3/4 c. cream
3/4 c. chicken stock
two 8 oz. walleye fillets
salt and pepper
1 tbsp. fresh parsley

» Place the butter in a heavy-bottomed pan; melt and continue to cook until butter is slightly browned and has a nutlike aroma.

» Add the mushrooms and cook over medium heat for about 5 minutes or until lightly browned.

» Add the leeks and cook a few more minutes.

» Add the sherry and cook a few minutes longer.

» Add the cream and chicken stock. Bring to a simmer and slip in the walleye fillets. Poach the fish for about 5 to 8 minutes, or until just done (check inside the fish).

» Gently remove the fish fillets to a warmed plate and cover lightly with foil.

» To finish, turn the heat to high and reduce the sauce until it's thick enough to coat a spoon. Swirl in the parsley and a little salt and pepper. Taste, adding more salt or a bit of lemon juice if needed.

« IN THE KITCHEN: The scene in a busy kitchen as Chef Lucia finishes poaching the fish and prepares to reduce the sauce for this recipe.

» COOK'S TIP: In this recipe, the combination of distinctive flavors complements the mild taste of walleye, and the slow addition of the ingredients one by one is what blends the flavors, peaking with the reduction of the sauce.

GUMBO!

A CREOLE SPECIALTY like this lies someplace between a soup and a stew, and is a perfect medium for the cook to experiment with: Add okra, tomatoes, garden greens, assorted sausages, and (if you're up to it) enough spice to make you cry!

To serve six generously . . .

1/2 lb. bacon, diced
2 to 3 tbsp. flour
1 c. each, onion, celery, green and red bell peppers, diced
1 clove garlic, chopped
1/4 tsp. cayenne (or to taste)
1/2 tsp. white pepper
1/2 tsp. dried thyme
1/2 tsp. dried oregano
8 c. chicken broth
1 lb. smoked sausage, sliced 3/4-inch thick into rounds
1 lb. fish, cut into one-inch cubes

» In a heavy-bottomed soup kettle over medium heat, cook the bacon until crispy. Remove the bacon with a slotted spoon, leaving the fat in the kettle. Reserve the bacon. Heat the bacon fat until it just begins to smoke, then add an equal amount of flour. Whisk until the mixture (roux) turns the color of a brown paper bag—a minimum of 10 minutes, but better as much as 30 minutes or more.

» Add the onion, celery, green and red bell peppers, garlic, cayenne, white pepper, thyme, oregano, the reserved bacon, and the chicken broth. Turn down the heat and cook gently for 15 minutes.

» Add the smoked sausage and the fish. Simmer gently for about 7 minutes. Season with salt and pepper and serve garnished with white rice.

« FISH TIP: Just about any sturdy fish works here, but those with firm, flakey flesh work especially well: stripers, catfish, sheepshead, burbot, as well as pike and bass. This is another good opportunity to use fish that have been frozen.

» COOK'S TIP: The secret to really good gumbo is the "roux," a mixture of flour and fat that thickens and flavors the dish. This gumbo calls for a dark roux which should be a deep, rich mahogany color. Beer—typically a lager—is the perfect complement to the heat of gumbo.

Fish and Potato
CHOWDER
with Hushpuppies

HEARTY CHOWDER is the perfect way to end a fishing weekend in fall or winter. Quit a little early. Fire up the fireplace. Gather friends around to relive the fishing and enjoy a toddy or hot cider. The chowder's served in just under an hour.

To serve six to eight . . .

8 slices thick-cut country bacon
1 large onion, chopped
1 stalk celery, chopped
1/4 c. flour
2 med. potatoes, peeled and cubed (same size as fish pieces)
4 c. fish or chicken stock
1 bay leaf
1/2 c. white wine
2 c. whole milk
salt and pepper
1/2 red and 1/2 green bell peppers,
    cored, seeded, and chopped
1 c. corn (frozen or fresh)
2 lbs. walleye fillets or other white fish, all bones removed,
    cut into about 1-in. cubes
fresh parsley

» In a large saucepan, sauté the bacon until crisp. Remove, drain on paper towels, and chop. From the pan, remove all but one tablespoon of the bacon fat, reserving the rest for the hushpuppies.

» To the pan, add the onion and celery and sauté until soft. Then sprinkle with flour, stirring constantly, and cook 3 to 4 minutes. Add the potatoes, stock, bay leaf, wine, milk, salt and pepper. Simmer about 20 minutes or until the potatoes are just soft.

» Add peppers, corn, and walleye and cook about 5 minutes or until the walleye is just tender—do not overcook.

» Spoon into bowls and garnish with parsley and the reserved chopped bacon. Serve with hushpuppies.

Hushpuppies . . .

1½ c. yellow cornmeal
1/2 c. flour
1 tsp. salt
1/2 tsp. sugar
2 tbsp. baking powder
1 tsp. baking soda
dash of cayenne
dash of black pepper

» Sift the ingredients together. Then add, combining with a spatula until just mixed:

2 eggs beaten and combined with enough buttermilk to
    equal 1¼ c.
2 tbsp. bacon fat
1/2 c. chopped scallion

» Heat the oil to 365°F and keep the temperature steady.

» Drop the mixture by tablespoons into the oil. Hushpuppies sink, then rise and turn over. After they rise to the surface, continue to cook for another minute or two. Remove with a slotted spoon and drain on paper towels.

» **COOK'S TIP:** Hushpuppies may be held in a low oven to keep warm but are best served at once. For extra flavor, sprinkle with a mixture of salt, pepper, and cayenne, or your favorite Cajun spices.

WALLEYE

Cioppino with Aioli Croutons

CIOPPINO originated in San Francisco, where the Italian immigrants would cook the catch of the day into this hearty soup. We finish our version with the garlicky mayonnaise called aioli. More than a soup but not quite a stew, it's wonderful made with most freshwater fish, but especially milder fish like walleye.

To serve six to eight . . .

2 tbsp. olive oil
1 c. onion, diced (or 1 c. fresh leeks, diced)
1 c. carrots, diced
1 tbsp. garlic, minced
1/2 c. fresh fennel, julienned
1/2 c. white wine
6 c. fish or chicken stock
1 c. sweet peppers, diced
1 c. tomatoes (fresh or canned), chopped
salt and pepper to taste
zest of 1/2 orange
1/2 tsp. saffron threads, toasted and crushed
1 lemon
3 lbs. walleye, cut into 1-inch cubes
1 tbsp. each fresh basil and parsley, chopped

» Place the olive oil in a large heavy soup pot. Over medium heat, sauté the onion, carrots, garlic, and fennel about 3 to 5 minutes. Add the wine and cook 3 minutes longer.

» Add the stock, along with the sweet peppers, tomatoes, salt and pepper, orange zest, and saffron. Cook for 8 to 10 minutes, stirring occasionally. Taste and adjust the seasoning by adding more salt and pepper or a squeeze of lemon. Add the walleye and simmer gently about 6 minutes or until just cooked. Don't overcook.

» Stir in the basil and parsley. Ladle the stew into warm bowls. Then float two croutons on top, along with a dollop of aioli.

« COOK'S TIP: Make this dish quickly so the bright colors, textures, and flavors are retained. Have all the ingredients ready, your hungry audience waiting. It also works well in the field, on a fly-in trip, or while out ice-fishing. Have everything cut up and ready in the cooler except your fresh catch, which is cut up and added at the last minute.

Croutons . . .

» Cut about 8 thin slices of French bread on a diagonal. Combine 1/4 cup olive oil with 1 teaspoon minced garlic and drizzle over the bread. Arrange on a cookie sheet and toast in a 350°F oven about 10 minutes, or until golden brown.

Aioli (Garlic Mayonnaise) . . .

This is a simple homemade mayonnaise made by cooking the egg yolks. It's far better-tasting than most commercial varieties and keeps for up to five days, covered, in the refrigerator.

3 egg yolks
dash of Tabasco sauce
2 tsp. Dijon mustard
1/4 tsp. each, salt and freshly ground pepper
3 tbsp. lemon juice (or vinegar)
2 c. vegetable oil
1 tbsp. (or more) minced garlic

» Put the egg yolks into the top of a double boiler and bring the water to a low simmer, whisking the yolks constantly.

» As the yolks begin to thicken, add Tabasco, mustard, salt, pepper, lemon juice, and garlic—continue whisking about 20 to 30 seconds, or until the mixture is thick and glossy and the yolks are cooked through to 130°F.

» Remove from heat and whisk in the oil: Begin drop by drop, then progress to a slow, steady stream. If the mixture is too thick, thin with a few drops of hot water. Taste and adjust the seasoning.

FISH CHOWDER
with Rouille & Croutons

DELICIOUS ON ITS OWN, this chowder is fabulous with a homemade rouille spread over a crispy crouton. The vegetables give this meal-in-a-bowl a light character, yet it's hearty as can be.

To serve four . . .

3 tbsp. olive oil
1 c. carrot, diced
1 c. onion, diced
1 c. celery, diced
1/2 c. leek, diced
1 tbsp. garlic, minced
1/2 c. fresh fennel, diced
1/2 c. red wine
4 c. chicken stock
4 c. clam juice (or another 4 c. of chicken stock)
1 16-oz. can diced tomatoes or 2 c. fresh tomatoes
1 bay leaf
salt and pepper
1 tbsp. fresh thyme (or 1 tsp. dried)
1½ lbs. fish in bite-size pieces
8 slices French bread (2 per person)
olive oil to brush on bread
rouille
fresh parsley, chopped fine for garnish

» Place the olive oil in a heavy soup pot over medium heat. When hot, add the carrot, onion, celery, leek, garlic, and fennel. Cover, and cook over low heat about 10 minutes, stirring occasionally. Add the wine and cook 5 minutes longer.

» Add the clam juice, chicken stock, tomatoes, bay leaf, salt and pepper, and thyme. Cook the mixture uncovered about 20 minutes.

» Add the fish and cook 12 to 15 minutes at a low simmer. Taste the broth and adjust the seasoning, adding more wine, salt, and pepper as needed. Serve in bowls with toasted French bread spread with rouille and sprinkled with chopped parsley.

This rouille is a variation on garlic mayonnaise, the classic French aioli, with puréed red bell pepper and a pinch of cayenne:

The rouille . . .

1 red bell pepper
3 egg yolks
dash of Tabasco sauce
1 to 2 tsp. Dijon mustard
1/4 tsp. each, salt and freshly ground pepper
1 tsp. cayenne powder, or to taste
4 cloves garlic, peeled and mashed to a paste
1 tbsp. lemon juice or vinegar
1½ to 2 c. olive oil

» First, prepare the red pepper purée. Rub the whole pepper with a little olive oil. Place on a cookie sheet and roast at 350°F for about 45 minutes. Allow to cool. Peel the skin off the pepper, then cut in half and remove all the seeds. Place the pepper in a blender or food processor and purée smooth. Set aside.

» Place the egg yolks in the top of a double boiler and bring the water to a low simmer, whisking the eggs constantly.

» As the eggs begin to thicken, add the Tabasco sauce, mustard, salt, pepper, cayenne, mashed garlic, lemon juice, and the reserved red pepper purée. Continue whisking about 20 to 30 seconds or until the mixture is thick and glossy and the eggs are cooked through to 130°F.

» Transfer the mixture to a food processor or blender. Add the oil in a slow steady stream. If the mixture is too thick, thin with a few drops of warm water or stock. Taste and add more salt or cayenne as desired. Refrigerate if not using immediately.

WALLEYE
and Potato Stew with Herbed Biscuits

HERE'S ANOTHER take on fish-and-potato stew that's always delicious and filling, popular with just about everyone. It's an easy one, too, although it takes a little time. Instead of the walleye, you can use any nice white-fleshed fish—catfish, pike, or bass.

To serve four . . .

1 tbsp. butter
2 strips bacon, cut small
1 med. onion, diced
2 stalks celery with leaves, diced
2 carrots, diced
3 cloves garlic, minced
1 tbsp. fresh thyme (or 1½ tsp. dried)
4 med. potatoes, diced
2 tbsp. flour
2 c. chicken stock
2 c. milk
1 c. heavy cream
1/4 c. dry white wine
dash of Tabasco sauce
salt and pepper to taste
1 lb. fish, cut into 1-inch pieces
juice of 1/2 lemon
2 tbsp. fresh parsley, finely chopped

» Place the butter and bacon in a heavy saucepan. Cook over medium heat until the bacon starts to brown. Add the onion, celery, carrot, garlic, thyme, and potatoes and cook covered, stirring often, for about 10 minutes.

» Add the flour and cook 2 to 3 more minutes. Add the chicken stock, milk, cream, wine, Tabasco sauce, and salt and pepper. Cook the stew uncovered, stirring often—for about 25 to 30 minutes or until the potatoes are tender.

» Toss the fish with the lemon and parsley and gently stir into the stew. Just simmer another 10 to 12 minutes, stirring gently until the fish is tender. Serve at once in big bowls with herbed biscuits.

Herbed biscuits . . .

2 c. flour
1 tbsp. baking powder
1/2 tsp. salt
a pinch of sugar
2 tbsp. mixed fresh herbs, chopped (try parsley, chives, dill)
2 c. heavy cream

» Preheat the oven to 350°F. Combine the flour, baking powder, salt, herbs, and sugar in a mixing bowl.

» With the mixer on low (or stirring by hand), slowly add the cream and mix just until combined.

» Drop by tablespoons onto a greased cookie sheet.

» Bake about 15 minutes or until golden and tender. Serve at once.

« FISH TIP: Largemouth bass are a popular sportfish that often are released. In many cases, though, they're so abundant in smaller sizes that they should be harvested to speed the growth of remaining fish. They go well in stews.

» COOK'S TIP: The herbed biscuits are so good and so easy to make that you'll probably want to use them with other dishes. Really, they go well with just about any fish dish, or can be used to complement a green salad or coleslaw. They would also be a good, lighter substitute for the heavier hushpuppies that are traditional fare with many deep-fried recipes. For a sweeter breakfast biscuit, omit the herbs, add 4 tablespoons of sugar, and 1/2 cup of dried fruit of your choice: currants, raisins, or chopped apricots. Eat warm, smothered with butter and preserves.

Tomato and
FISH SOUP
with Pasta

I LOVE THIS SOUP, one of the most adaptable options I've found—easy to reheat, when it tastes perhaps even better. Just make sure you only reheat to a simmer.

Virtually any fish works—usually a firm, white-fleshed fish like pike, walleye, or burbot (eelpout), but also trout or salmon. Serve with French bread or croutons. Drizzling additional olive oil over the soup just before serving is a tasty touch.

To serve four . . .

3 tbsp. olive oil
1 lg. onion, chopped
3 cloves garlic, minced
2 stalks celery, chopped
1 leek, chopped
4 tomatoes, chopped
pinch of saffron
1 tbsp. fresh thyme (or 1 tsp. dried)
1/2 c. white wine
6 c. chicken stock
salt and pepper
2 oz. vermicelli, broken into 2-inch lengths
2 c. firm-fleshed fish, cut into bite-sized pieces
2 tbsp. fresh parsley, chopped
1 tbsp. fresh basil, chopped (or 1 tsp. dried)
French bread or croutons (optional)

» Heat the olive oil in a heavy stock pot. Add the onion, garlic, celery, and leek, and cook over low heat 10 minutes, stirring occasionally.

» Add the tomatoes, saffron, thyme, wine, stock, and salt and pepper to taste. Cook at a low simmer for about 1/2 hour to allow the flavors to develop.

» Add the vermicelli and cook 10 minutes, or until tender but not quite done. Next, add the fish and cook an additional 8 minutes or so. Stir in the parsley and basil.

« **FISH TIP:** Paddlefish are plankton feeders that must be snagged to be harvested. These primitive fish (no bones—only cartilage) make good table fare when properly cleaned and prepared, as in a soup like this one.

» **COOK'S TIP:** This is another perfect option to take with you chilled into the field. Add cubed fresh fish after the soup's been reheated. Simmer another 8 minutes for a hearty, healthful shorelunch.

Hearty
CHOWDER

THE IDEA IS TO USE the best of your own local fresh ingredients, given the season: In autumn add some garden squash and a pinch of sage, and in winter, enrich the ingredients with a splash of cream and some white beans. For spring, substitute the corn and peppers with 1-inch pieces of fresh asparagus and some wild mushrooms, if you're lucky enough to find them.

To serve eight as a first course; entrées for four . . .

4 oz. bacon
1 lg. onion, chopped
1 stalk celery, chopped
1/4 c. unbleached all-purpose flour
2 med. potatoes, peeled and diced
2 c. homemade chicken broth or low-salt canned broth
1 bay leaf
2 c. whole milk
1/2 red and 1/2 green bell peppers, cored, seeded, and chopped
4 or 5 ears sweetcorn—shucked, with kernels cut from the cob to equal about 3 c. (or substitute frozen corn)
salt and pepper
1½ lbs. fish, cut into 1-inch pieces
fresh chives, basil, or parsley, chopped, to equal about 1 tbsp. (use one herb or a combination)

» In a large, heavy soup kettle, fry the bacon until crisp. Remove the bacon. In the same pot with the bacon fat, add the onion and celery and cook over medium heat until soft. Meanwhile, chop the bacon and reserve.

» Sprinkle the flour over the vegetables, stirring and cooking for about 3 to 4 minutes. Add the potatoes, chicken stock, bay leaf, and a sprinkle of salt and pepper, then bring the mixture to a boil. Immediately reduce the heat and simmer until the potatoes are soft, about 20 minutes.

» Add the milk, bell peppers, corn, and the fish. Cook the soup at a simmer for 8 to 10 minutes—don't let it boil. Adjust the seasoning, adding salt and pepper to taste and perhaps a dash of Tabasco sauce or a splash of wine. Just before serving, stir in the bacon and the herbs—or sprinkle them on top.

« FISH TIP: The In-Fisherman staff finds something to fish for 365 days a year, on ice and on open water. Dress right for the situation, whether the temperature's -30°F on ice, or 10°F for a river trip for walleyes or steelhead on open water.

» COOK'S TIP: This is a recipe that works with mild-tasting fish—walleye, burbot (eelpout), crappies, white bass (pictured), bluegills, and perch. Striper would be excellent, as would smaller largemouth bass. I often use frozen fish here. Be sure to date fish when you freeze them.

Tomato-Basil Fish
CHOWDER
with Garlic Croutons

THE FISH OF CHOICE may vary from delicate walleye or crappie to the more distinctive salmon or trout; the croutons are traditional and go well with any fish soup. Try this on any chilly night, or in summer with fresh garden tomatoes and basil.

To serve four . . .

2 tbsp. olive oil
2 stalks celery, coarsely chopped
1 onion, coarsely chopped
1 carrot, peeled and coarsely chopped
1 med. green bell pepper, chopped
1 jalapeño pepper, finely chopped
2 cloves garlic, mashed
5-6 large ripe tomatoes, peeled, cored, and chopped (or one 12-oz. can of diced tomatoes)
3-4 c. chicken broth (depends on how juicy your tomatoes are)
salt and pepper
a splash of balsamic vinegar
3 fish fillets, about 8 oz. each, deboned and cut into 1-inch squares
a big handful of fresh basil, washed and chopped
croutons

» In a large, heavy soup kettle, heat the olive oil and add the celery, onion, carrot, peppers, and garlic. Cook over medium heat, covered, for about 10 minutes, stirring occasionally.

» Add tomatoes, broth, salt, pepper, and vinegar. Cook over medium heat another 15 minutes.

» Add the fish and simmer gently for 8 to 10 minutes, so the fish is cooked through but not falling apart.

» Divide the basil into four bowls. Ladle the fish soup over the basil and garnish with croutons.

« FISH TIP: No respect? In places like Minnesota, the wonderfully firm, mild-tasting flesh of the burbot (ling, eelpout, lawyer) is beginning to be recognized as fine tablefare. In many other places across North America, the fish has been a popular table fish for years. Be sure to trim the gray, fatty flesh from the outside of the fillet.

» COOK'S TIP: **Garlic Croutons**—Cut 1/2 loaf of French bread into small cubes. Generously drizzle with a mixture of olive oil and melted butter, and mix with a couple of cloves of mashed garlic. Spread the croutons on a baking sheet and bake for about 10 minutes at 425°F, shaking the pan every few minutes until the croutons are golden brown and crisp.

FISH SOUP
Provençal with Lemon Aioli & Crouton

THIS SOUP has a few ingredients to gather, but it's easy to prepare and sure to be a favorite as a first course for a dinner or as the main course. This also is a nice one to make ahead at home, chill, and then take out onto the ice or into the field, where fresh fish can be added after the soup's been reheated over a fire.

To serve four . . .

1/4 c. olive oil
1 lg. yellow onion, chopped
1 leek, washed and chopped
1 c. mixed bell peppers, diced
1 carrot, peeled and diced small
4 cloves garlic, chopped fine
1 potato, peeled and cut into 1-inch pieces
1 c. white wine
4 c. chicken stock
4 c. tomatoes, peeled, seeded, and diced
1 tsp. dried basil
1 tsp. dried thyme
1 tsp. fennel seeds, toasted and crushed
a few shots of Tabasco and Worcestershire sauce
salt and pepper
1 lb. walleye, bass, pike, or burbot (eelpout) fillets, deboned
   and cut into one-inch chunks

» Heat the olive oil in a heavy-bottomed pot over medium heat. Add the onions, leeks, carrot, peppers, garlic, and potatoes and cook over medium heat for 8 to 10 minutes or until they begin to soften.

» Add the wine, stock, tomatoes, salt and pepper, Tabasco, Worcestershire, and herbs. Cook over low heat for about 30 minutes, or until the potatoes are soft and the flavors have blended.

» Add the fish and simmer about 10 minutes or until it's tender.

» Taste the soup and add lemon or salt, or more Tabasco if desired. Serve the soup in bowls with a big crouton and a dollop of lemon aioli.

Lemon Aioli...

2 egg yolks
1 clove garlic
salt and pepper
1 teaspoon lemon juice
zest from one lemon
few drops each of Tabasco and Worcestershire sauce
3/4 c. olive oil
1/4 c. vegetable oil

» In a blender, add all the ingredients except the oils and the zest of lemon.

» With the blender running, drop by drop slowly add the oils so the yolks absorb them. Thin down the mixture if necessary by adding droplets of warm water.

» Remove from the blender, fold in the zest, and season with more salt and pepper if necessary.

» COOK'S TIP: Several recipes in this book (see Walleye Cioppino with Aioli) suggest crouton preparations. Another easy version begins by slicing hard bread on a bias, about one inch thick. Fry the bread in a bit of olive oil over medium-high heat until browned on each side.

Classic
FISH SALAD
Sandwich

RECIPES LIKE THIS are so easy to make, and so delicious, I'm always surprised they aren't used more often. For this particular mix of ingredients, a mild-flavored white-fleshed fish works best. Walleye's a favorite, but crappies, bass, bluegills, and perch are fine. Properly frozen fish also work well in a salad or salad-sandwich like this.

To serve two . . .

    two 8-oz. fish fillets, cooked and flaked
    1 rib celery, diced
    1 small onion, diced
    1/2 c. mayonnaise
    2 sweet pickles, chopped
    squeeze of lemon juice
    salt and pepper to taste

» Mix the ingredients together and layer on toasted bread, along with tomato, lettuce, and onion.

» **COOK'S TIP:** During summer, use this salad in combination with fresh melon like cantaloupe. One approach is to buy small ripe melons, halve them, remove the seeds, and place a large dollop of the salad in the melon. This salad also makes a nice appetizer served in small portions on croutons or toasted French bread (see recipes in this book).

« **COOK'S TIP:** This is a wonderful sandwich spread to take with you when fishing. I prefer to make sandwiches in the field, so I bring bread and keep the spread in a container until it's lunchtime. I like a chewy, crusty rye or a heavy, coarse wheat bread. If you make sandwiches at home, slip them into a locking plastic bag and store them in a plastic container so they don't get squashed. This shot is from the bakery at Lucia's.

Cold Poached
TROUT
with Lemon, Mint and a Tabouleh Salad

I LOVE this simple dish and I know you will too. I prepare it the evening after that first trout trip of spring and slip it into the refrigerator to be enjoyed the next noon as a light lunch, or the next evening for supper. I serve it with a tabouleh salad and French bread, along with a chilled pinot grigio or sauvignon blanc.

Trout to serve four . . .

2 lemons, sliced
1/2 c. fresh mint leaves
dash of black pepper
1 garlic clove, peeled and crushed
dash of white wine or vinegar
4 whole trout, cleaned and gutted

» Combine all the above except the trout in a deep pan or fish poacher with 2 quarts of water. Bring to a simmer.

» Gently slide in the trout and cook at a gentle simmer for 8 to 10 minutes, or until tender. Turn off the heat and, with spatulas, carefully remove the trout. Chill.

Tabouleh salad . . .

1 c. bulgur wheat
1½ c. boiling water

» Combine the wheat and boiling water—remove from stove, let sit to absorb the water and cool. Toss with the dressing (below). Add fresh chopped mint, red onions, cucumber, tomatoes, parsley, salt and pepper.

Dressing for tabouleh . . .

In a blender combine:

1/4 c. vinegar or lemon juice
1 clove garlic, peeled and crushed
1 tbsp. smooth Dijon mustard
zest of 1 lemon
dash of salt and pepper
1 generous tbsp. fresh mint, chopped (6 to 10 large leaves)

» Place all the ingredients in a blender.

» Blend for about 30 seconds. Keep the blender running.

Then add:
3/4 c. oil

» Add the oil in a slow, steady stream. If the dressing is too thick, add a few drops of water.

» Taste, adjust seasoning, and chill.

» Presentation: Place a few lettuce leaves on a plate. Put the trout on top and then the tabouleh on the side. Garnish with a wedge of lemon and a fresh mint sprig.

« FISH TIP: During summer, trout in some lakes and reservoirs seek refuge in deeper water below the thermocline. Use a temperature probe to find water below about 55°F. Trout like this cutthroat from mountain lakes usually stay shallower year-round.

» COOK'S TIP: For a different flavor, try the mustard vinaigrette from the Walleye Salad Niçoise for this preparation.

WALLEYE

Salad Niçoise

JUDGING BY RESPONSE from *In-Fisherman* readers, this is the most popular salad the magazine has featured over the years. A North Country twist on the famous French salad, I love the way this recipe uses the bounty of the summer garden after a day of fishing: basil, tomatoes, potatoes, beans and lettuce. In cooler months, I make this a smaller first course or side salad, with a warming soup and some toasty bread.

To serve four . . .

4 walleye fillets, 5 or 6 ounces each
2 heads fresh lettuce (oak/Boston/butter)
1/4 lb. fresh green beans, blanched in boiling water, cooled, and drained
1/2 red onion, sliced thin
fresh basil leaves (wash and pat dry)
4 hardboiled eggs, peeled and halved
pitted black olives
small new potatoes, boiled and chilled
tomatoes or cherry tomatoes
capers (about 2 tbsp.)
2 tbsp. fresh parsley, chopped

» Place the walleye fillets in a roasting pan. Sprinkle with salt and pepper and drizzle with olive oil. Add enough water to film the bottom of the pan.

» Bake at 350° F for about 10 to 12 minutes, or until cooked (don't overcook). Chill the fillets.

» Place a bed of lettuce and basil on each of 4 plates. Arrange the walleye fillet and the other ingredients onto each plate. Drizzle on the dressing to taste (you can prepare this in advance), and sprinkle with parsley.

Mustard Vinaigrette (can be prepared in advance) . . .

1/4 c. shallots, peeled and sliced
1/2 c. white wine vinegar
2 tbsp. Dijon mustard
3/4 c. extra virgin olive oil
salt and freshly ground pepper

» Place the shallots in a medium bowl and add the vinegar. The vinegar marinates and tenderizes the shallots, giving the vinaigrette a light, distinctive flavor. Allow it to sit for about 2 hours at room temperature.

» Whisk in the mustard, then add the oil in a slow, steady stream as you continue to whisk. Season with salt and pepper.

» **COOK'S TIP:** In the winter make a smaller salad, using whatever looks bright and fresh, and accompany it with a hearty bowl of split pea soup. Or serve as a smaller first course before a roast chicken dinner.

» **COOK'S TIP:** This method of cooking fish is useful for salads (as above), fish spreads, or simply a lighter-style presentation that can be complemented with one of our Delicate Herb Butters or a dollop of tartar sauce. When baking, add a splash of white wine to the liquid for more flavor. To test if the fish is done, gently pull it apart with a fork—it should flake easily.

« **FISH TIP:** This is another recipe where a little-bit-larger walleye would work as well as smaller fish. Simply adjust the cooking time slightly. The fillets from a 4- or 5-pound fish would serve four. I recommend using only freshly caught fish, here.

CRAPPIE

BLT Sandwich with Herb Mayonnaise

THE CLASSIC BLT gets a new and delicious twist by adding a crispy crappie fillet. Serve it with homemade herb mayo on lightly toasted bread with a side of chips or potato salad. This is a fine lunch after a morning on the water.

For each sandwich . . .

Prepare in advance:
herb mayonnaise

Then:
1/2 c. flour
salt and pepper
small pinch of cayenne
butter or bacon fat for frying the fish
1 crappie (or other fish) fillet
2 slices good sandwich bread
iceberg lettuce
2 slices thick bacon, cooked
sliced fresh tomatoes

» Combine the flour, salt, pepper, and cayenne. Dust each fillet in the flour mixture.

» Heat the butter or bacon fat in a sauté pan until almost smoking. Sauté each fillet about 4 minutes on each side, until crisp and golden.

» Toast the bread and spread with the mayonnaise. Layer on the tomato, lettuce, and bacon.

» Place the fillet on top of the bacon and top with the bread.

Herb mayonnaise...

2 tbsp. fresh lemon juice
1 tbsp. Dijon mustard
1 tsp. salt
1/2 tsp. white pepper
1 egg
few drops of Tabasco sauce
few drops of Worcestershire sauce
1/2 c. vegetable oil
1/2 c. olive oil
2 tbsp. mixed and chopped fresh herbs (parsley, tarragon, chives)

» Put all ingredients except the oils in the bowl of a food processor fitted with a metal blade. Process.

» With the motor running, slowly pour in the oil in a steady stream. Thin the mayo with a few drops of warm water if it seems too thick.

» Stir in the herbs; add salt, pepper, and lemon to taste.

« FISH TIP: Many anglers believe that panfish like crappies and bluegills are the finest-tasting fish of all. Practice selective harvest with panfish, too, keeping the more plentiful smaller to medium fish and leaving larger ones to sustain good fishing.

» COOK'S TIP: The key to making mayonnaise is to add the oil very slowly. If the mayo gets too thick, add a few drops of warm water then continue with the oil. Vary the herbs in the recipe for a change of flavor, or you can omit them for a simple mayonnaise.

Cocktail
Menu
Ask your SERVER about the FEATURED DRINK of
CLASSIC MARTINI
Belvedere Vodka or Boodles Gin,
Dry Vermouth, Olive or a Lemon Twist
MANHATTAN
Knob Creek Bourbon,
Sweet Vermouth, Maraschino Ch
OLD FASHIONED
Knob Creek Bourbon,
Sugar Cube, Muddled O
Served on the Rocks, V
ROB ROY
Dewars Scotc
Sweet Vermouth
MARGARIT
Patron T
Cointrea
GIMI
Boo
Fr

Smoked
SALMON
Sandwich with Sprouts

LIGHTLY SMOKED TROUT including steelhead work here, too—or instead use fresh salmon or trout, either poached or baked. Serve spread on a chewy black bread topped with alfalfa sprouts or watercress and radish slices. It's a fine sandwich during any season, and it's good as an appetizer served in smaller portions on crackers or spread on small pieces of toasted French bread.

To serve one . . .

1/4 lb. cooked fish
1/4 c. sour cream
juice of 1/2 lemon
finely grated peel of one lemon
1/2 tbsp. fresh dill or chives
salt and pepper
dash of Tabasco and Worcestershire sauce
pinch of cayenne

» Blend all ingredients in a food processor. Spread on bread and garnish with sprouts.

« COOK'S TIP: A nice salad can be made by using a vinaigrette with a combination of sliced scallions, tomatoes, and other seasonal vegetables.

» HARVEST TIP: During spring and early summer, watercress often can be found in springs or tiny rivulets connected to trout streams. The perfect harvest day for me is a few fresh trout for an evening meal, accompanied by morel mushrooms found along the stream, and a fresh watercress salad. Rinse watercress thoroughly under cold running water, shake out the water, and rinse again.

Smoked Fish
MOUSSE

MOUSSE CAN EASILY be made ahead of time for entertaining at a moment's notice. It makes a wonderful appetizer at holiday gatherings. Smoked whitefish has a particularly firm texture and a delicate flavor, but any smoked fish works. Salmon, with its pink color, is a favorite. This is simple and delicious.

To serve eight . . .

3 oz. smoked fish
1 c. cream cheese
1 tbsp. lemon juice
1 tsp. grated onion
1/2 tsp. salt
1/4 tsp. white pepper
dash of Tabasco sauce
whole milk (or half and half) as needed
1 tbsp. fresh chives, snipped

» Remove all the bones from the fish. Place the fish and all the ingredients except chives and milk into a food processor with a steel blade. Blend until smooth. Thin the mixture with a little whole milk (or half and half), if necessary.

» Fold in the chives. Turn the mousse into a serving bowl; serve it with crackers or croutons and fresh vegetables, and perhaps fruit such as apples.

« **COOK'S TIP:** This mousse makes a wonderful seasonal presentation: In spring, serve it spread on crackers with an asparagus tip and a watercress sprig; in summer, on French bread with a slice of garden tomato and, in the fall, smudge the mousse on crisp apple and pear slices.

» **COOK'S TIP:** Part of the key to the success of any dish is visual. The tablecloth, napkin, plate, and an appealing combination of colors bring an aura of pleasant expectation before the first bite. Fresh peaches work well in salads, salsas, and as a simple "side."

MARINADES
for Grilled Fish

IT DOESN'T MATTER if you have walleye fillets, salmon steaks, or dressed rainbow trout: Fire up the grill and use one of these light, fresh marinades to spice up the catch. Marinades also work well for broiling. And they can be a delicious change-of-pace used before dusting fillets or fish steaks and pan-frying or deep-frying.

Each recipe is enough for about four fillets:

Orange-honey marinade . . .

fillets, steaks, or whole fish
grated zest of 2 oranges
1½ c. fresh orange juice
1/4 c. balsamic vinegar
2 tbsp. honey
1 tbsp. soy sauce
1 tbsp. crushed, chopped garlic

Lemon-ginger marinade . . .

1/2 c. lemon juice
2 med. garlic cloves, minced
1 tbsp. fresh ginger, minced
1/4 c. olive oil
1/4 c. vegetable oil

» Make each marinade by whisking together the ingredients and pouring over the fish. Marinate for about an hour.

» Brush grill grates with vegetable oil and grill the fish over medium-hot coals, basting frequently with the marinade. The honey forms a glaze as the fish cooks.

» Do not overcook the fish. Most 8- to 10-ounce fillets require no more than 6 or 7 minutes, cooked on just one side. Larger fillets may need to be turned (I turn one-inch-thick steaks once). Apply the general rule of cooking fish: 8 minutes total per inch of fish, so an inch-thick whole trout usually requires about 4 minutes per side.

« COOK'S TIP: To grill whole fish, place a sprig of thyme, a slice of lemon, and a generous sprinkle of salt and pepper into each cavity before cooking the fish. Here, I add corn to the fire before preparing to grill fish for an In-Fisherman Television segment.

» COOK'S TIP: When marinating fish for longer than about 30 minutes, place in the refrigerator. Don't save marinades for later use; prepare them fresh each time. These can also be drizzled over a plain baked fish before serving, much like a sauce. This preparation is good served cold, too, so if you have plenty of fish, grill extra for tomorrow's sandwich.

Tequila-Cured
GRAVLAX

GRAVLAX IS A SALT- AND SUGAR-CURED delicacy originally from Scandinavia (lax means salmon in Swedish), where it's the custom to start the morning with thinly shaved pieces heaped on a plate and served with small shots of aquavit. This recipe uses brown sugar with lime and tequila for a fresh, clean flavor.

Thinly slice the salmon (or steelhead trout) and use as appetizers on crackers spread with cream cheese or sour cream; in scrambled eggs or omelets; on toast, or in sandwiches. This is a wonderful addition to any buffet, a fresh alternative to smoked salmon or trout.

To serve four to six . . .

3 generous tbsp. fresh dill, chopped
3 generous tbsp. shallots or white end of scallions, chopped
3 generous tbsp. fresh parsley, chopped
zest of 3 limes, chopped
1- to 2-lb. side of salmon, skinned and boned

» Combine the ingredients except the salmon. Sprinkle them equally on both sides of the salmon. Cover a cookie sheet with plastic wrap and place the salmon on it.

Next, combine:
juice of 3 limes
2 c. brown sugar
3 c. kosher salt
3/4 c. tequila

» Pack this mixture on both sides of the salmon. Cover the top of the salmon with waxed paper.

» Place a cookie sheet atop the waxed paper, weight it down with several 16-oz. cans from the cupboard or some other modestly heavy objects, and refrigerate for 24 hours.

» Drain off liquid and gently flip both cookie sheets so the salmon is reversed. Weight down again and refrigerate another 24 hours.

» The salmon should feel firm—almost stiff. (For extra-thick salmon, or if it doesn't feel firm and stiff, cure with weights for another 24 to 48 hours.)

» Quickly and gently run the salmon under ice-cold water to remove the brine. Pat the fish completely dry with paper towels.

» Keep refrigerated. Serve cut into paper-thin slices.

« **FISH TIP:** Gravlax really brings out the pure flavor of the fish, so I always like to use fresh fish. The texture, color, and size of king salmon make this fish my favorite here, but steelhead are delicious, too. Gravlax keeps for up to two weeks in the refrigerator. Wrap tightly in freezer-grade plastic wrap.

» **COOK'S TIP:** Gravlax is a wonderful and versatile staple: For canapés, slice thin on rye crackers with mustard mixed with fresh chopped dill and a little minced red onion. For lunch, try a good pasta with a drizzle of olive oil, shaved gravlax, and a dollop of sour cream with lemon. For a side dish, slices of gravlax on a watercress salad with cooked sliced beets and a sprinkle of horseradish; and for an elegant first course, a tiny baked new potato with a slice of gravlax and a garnish of sour cream, really good with Champagne in lieu of the classic aquavit. Lastly, thin rye bread with lemon garlic mayonnaise and a thin tomato slice on gravlax makes a terrific lunch.

Delicate Herb
BUTTERS

HERB BUTTERS are a delicate complement to fish, whether the fish is pan-fried, broiled, grilled, or poached. I like the basil-oregano blend on salmon, the dill with walleye, and the cilantro on catfish—but you'll want to experiment.

Brush the butters on during cooking or, more commonly, add a spoonful on or alongside the fish just before serving. Each recipe yields enough for about four.

Basil-oregano butter . . .

In a small mixing bowl, beat together 1/2 cup softened butter, 1 tbsp. dry sherry, 2 tbsp. snipped fresh basil, 2 tbsp. fresh oregano, 1/2 tsp. minced garlic, and a dash of salt and black pepper. Refrigerate, covered, for several hours. Soften the butter before serving.

Cilantro butter . . .

In a small mixing bowl, beat together 1/2 cup softened butter, 1/4 cup fresh cilantro, 3 tbsp. lime juice, zest from 2 limes, 1 tsp. minced garlic, 1/8 tsp. salt, 1/8 tsp. white pepper, and a big dash of Tabasco sauce. Refrigerate covered for several hours. Soften the butter before serving.

Dill butter . . .

In a small mixing bowl, beat together 1/2 cup softened butter with 1 tbsp. dry white wine, 3 tbsp. fresh dill, 1 tbsp. fresh parsley, 1 tsp. minced onion, 2 tsp. lemon juice, and a dash of salt and black pepper. Refrigerate covered for several hours. Soften the butter before serving.

« FISHING TIP: On a fly-in trip where you're doing the cooking, these butters, prepared at home and transported via cooler into camp, make any meal of fish a delight. Cook your cleaned fish in a little bacon fat over a smoky fire, add some sliced potatoes, and a chunk of one of these butters—delicious!

» COOK'S TIP: These versatile butters freeze wonderfully, so make extra for a quick meal. Try them on grilled steak and baked chicken, too.

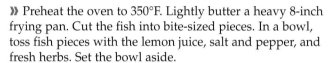

Smoked Trout
FRITTATA

IN ITALY, frittatas often are picnic food. They make a nice dish for breakfast or brunch, and are a midnight treat that can be eaten hot or at room temperature. They reheat well, so make extra. For a condiment, try a little sour cream mixed with a bit of horseradish. Frittatas are so easy to make, I predict you'll love this recipe.

To serve six . . .

4 oz. smoked fish
1 tsp. lemon juice
salt and pepper
1 tsp. fresh thyme or tarragon, chopped
8 whole eggs, plus 3 egg whites
dash Tabasco sauce
3 c. heavy cream
1 tbsp. chopped fresh parsley
3/4 c. cream cheese
sour cream and horseradish (optional)

» Preheat the oven to 350°F. Lightly butter a heavy 8-inch frying pan. Cut the fish into bite-sized pieces. In a bowl, toss fish pieces with the lemon juice, salt and pepper, and fresh herbs. Set the bowl aside.

» Mix together the eggs, egg whites, Tabasco sauce, and heavy cream. Beat lightly.

» Pour half of the batter into the prepared pan. Sprinkle the fish over the mixture and pour the remaining mixture into the pan. It should be just below the rim of the pan. Sprinkle with the parsley and blob on the cream cheese.

» Bake about 40 minutes, until the top is set solid when the pan is lightly shaken. Slice inside with a knife, to be sure—the knife should come out clean.

» Cool slightly, turn the pan over onto a board or serving platter and remove the frittata. Cut into wedges.

《 FISH TIP: Whitefish (pictured left) and the ciscoes (pictured right), so often caught through the ice during winter, also smoke up nicely and work well in this recipe.

》 COOK'S TIP: Smoked fish makes this recipe distinctive, but it also can be made with cooked trout or salmon that are not smoked. Smoking is a wonderful and ancient way of preserving fish. If you don't smoke your own fish, be sure you buy a high-quality product, one that uses only salt, fish, and real smoke in their product. Talk to your fish seller so you know what you're buying.

SALSAS for Fish

THESE ARE A REFRESHING change of pace that can be paired with any sautéed, poached, or baked fish, but they're particularly good with grilled fish. The orange and black-bean salsa is my favorite, and the cranberry salsa will surprise you. It's delicious.

The mango-habañero is for those of you who like "a good swift kick in your salsa!" Most of us need to tone that one down a notch by using jalapeños in place of the habañeros. The quality of the mango has a lot to do with how that recipe turns out. Each of these recipes serves four.

Orange and black-bean salsa...

one 15-oz. can cooked black beans
2 oranges, peeled, seeded, and cut into small sections
2 jalapeño peppers cut into rounds
1/2 red bell pepper, diced
1/4 red onion, diced
1 c. fresh cilantro, chopped
1 tbsp. olive oil
1 tbsp. vinegar
salt and pepper
1/2 tsp. toasted and ground cumin

» Drain the black beans. Combine all ingredients and taste for final seasoning.

Mango habañero salsa...

Note: Wear gloves when you handle the habañero chili!

1 small red onion, finely diced
2 cloves garlic, minced
1 ripe mango, diced small
1/2 c. fresh cilantro, chopped
juice and zest of one lime
1/4 habañero chili (or 1/2 jalapeño pepper, seeded and finely chopped)
salt to taste
1 tbsp. olive oil

» Combine all ingredients and taste for seasoning.

Cranberry salsa...

1 c. fresh or frozen cranberries
1 tbsp. grated ginger
2 cloves garlic
1 jalapeño pepper, seeded
juice and zest of 1/2 lime
4 to 5 tbsp. sugar (or to taste)
1/4 c. fresh cilantro, chopped
2 scallions chopped rough

» Put all ingredients into a food processor and chop fine.

« FISH TIP: So begins another day on the river. Anticipation runs high. These salsas would go well with that planned shorelunch, as the flavors get even better the next day and taste good on any kind of fish.

» SERVING TIP: These easy salsas are a wonderful appetizer served with big, salty chips. Or, even better, serve with deep-fried fish fingers, or any crispy fried-fish recipe. Because of the robust flavors of the salsas, traditional Pilsner beers are a nice complement.

BUTTER SAUCE

for Baked, Grilled or Sautéed Fish

IT'S WONDERFUL to savor the unique flavor of the fish species you've been lucky enough to catch. I often add just a simple sauce like this to complement and expand on the natural flavor. The fillets here have been dusted in lightly seasoned flour then sautéed over medium-high heat in a little oil and butter, but this sauce is delicious with a lightly poached fish, too.

The butter sauce (enough for about six portions) . . .

1/2 lb. butter
1 small red onion, chopped (1/2 c.)
1/2 c. fresh parsley, chopped
1/2 c. fresh herbs (such as dill or tarragon), chopped
2 tbsp. capers
juice and zest from one lemon
salt and pepper

» Add the butter to a saucepan, melt, and continue cooking until it turns a golden brown and has a nut-like aroma.

» Add the remaining ingredients and cook over medium heat for several minutes. Spoon a little over the fish or serve it alongside.

« **PHOTOGRAPHER AT WORK:** Chuck Nelson works from a Polaroid black-and-white photo to add finishing touches just before shooting the final recipe pose, rearranging individual pieces of food and changing the lighting so the final version fits a magazine layout, typically a two-page spread, with room for the recipe far left or far right.

» **COOK'S TIP:** In classic French cooking, a lightly browned butter is a beurre noisette. The nutty flavor of the butter adds distinction to sautées. The butter often is flavored with capers, vinegar or lemon juice, and parsley.

WINE with Fish

SOME OF the best rules for pairing wine with food are from my favorite wine writer Karen MacNeil, in her book, *The Wine Bible.*

Rule one, which works wonderfully with the recipes in this book: *Pair great with great and humble with humble.* The Crappie BLT for example, and the simpler shorelunch recipes, goes well with an inexpensive white wine or an ice-cold beer. The poached salmon with butter sauce may merit a fine Champagne.

Rule two: *Match delicate to delicate and robust to robust.* The gumbos and Creole recipes here taste good with big spicy wines, like zinfandel; while a delicate wine, a nice Chablis or rosé, for example, goes well with the baked fish recipes or simple chowders.

Rule three: *Decide if you want to mirror a flavor or contrast it.* The flavors of the grilled catfish with sweetcorn sauce mirror a sweeter-style chenin blanc, while it contrasts sharply with a bone-dry Muscadet.

Finally: *Above all, don't complicate things.* Whatever you open, have fun, toast the meal, the fish, your friends—and enjoy life!

Fundamental
SHORELUNCH

FISH FRESHLY CAUGHT, harvested selectively, and cooked outdoors over a fire perfectly complete the circle of life we're living out there. Many anglers consider fish cooked like this to be the best they've ever eaten and the most memorable part of the trip.

Shorelunch is easy to do if you prepare for it. The fish doesn't always have to be cooked over an open fire. A Coleman stove on a picnic table at a campsite or on the tailgate of your truck works, too.

The classic shorelunch scene transpires about noon, on an island point somewhere in the wilderness, the fish freshly caught that morning, the fire built with wood gathered nearby. Or you've been on a river all day and have pulled onto a sandbar and gathered driftwood for the cooking fire, which becomes the campfire. Don't limit your imagination. A breakfast of fresh fish, bacon, and eggs, or the hash recipe included in this section, are perfect shoremeals.

Cooking over an open fire requires a larger fire reduced to a bed of coals. Control the heat by adding sticks or split wood about 1/2 inch in diameter. Be sure to have more than enough sticks piled up to get you through the cooking detail.

A cast-iron pan is the classic way to fry fish outdoors. I usually use a simple flour and cornmeal coating and fry the fillet in bacon fat or butter.

For deep-frying, use a 1- or 2-pound coffee can, saving its plastic top. Punch two holes on the top opposite edges of the can and use a wire coat hanger to make a handle. Remove any covering on the outside of the can, and heat it up well over an open flame at home to remove any other coatings it might have.

≈ A shore breakfast of bacon, eggs, and fresh fish.

Cool the can and add enough solid Crisco or lard to fill it half full. Put the plastic top back on the can. On a trip you can use, cool, and reuse this oil several times.

Crisco or lard works best because when it's cooled, it firms up again—no spilling. Also, deep-frying calls for oil temperatures in the 360°F range. Crisco and lard can stand temperatures up to 400°F, so they can take the range of temperatures that go with working over an open fire, where absolute control of the heat isn't possible.

« *In-Fisherman* Editor In Chief Doug Stange and Chef Lucia prepare to shoot an outdoor cooking scene for In-Fisherman Television, highlighting In-Fisherman's commitment to promoting the selective harvest of fish.

Tips for Deep-Frying...

» A wet batter must be ice-cold, so that when it hits the hot oil it instantly seals the batter around the fish, allowing the fish to cook by steaming within the firm, crunchy crust. The fish doesn't get soft and the batter doesn't get soggy.

» To seal batter properly around the fish, the oil must range between 360°F and 380°F. You can tell if the oil's ready by adding a drop of the batter to the oil. If the temperature's right, the batter bubbles profusely on the surface. If the batter's too warm or the oil's not hot enough, the batter just sits there, barely bubbling and turning soggy.

» Don't add so much fish at once that the oil temperature drops too low. Allow the oil to heat up again between batches of fish.

A Nice Wet Batter for Deep-Frying...

2 egg yolks
1 c. ice water
1½ c. seasoned flour (add salt & pepper and dried herbs, if you wish)

» Mix the egg yolk, water, and flour. Dip a small fillet or small portion of a larger fillet into the batter, let the excess run off, and slip the fillet portion into the oil.

My Favorite Dry Breading for Deep-Frying or Sautéeing...

flour seasoned with salt and pepper
a pinch of cayenne
dried herbs
garlic salt

« Lucia's favorite dry breading.

« The fire's reduced to coals and controlled by adding small pieces of wood.

Also prepare:

several beaten eggs with a little milk
cornmeal (or crushed cornflakes)

» Dip the clean fish fillet in the seasoned flour, then in the egg mix. Allow the excess egg to drip off, then dip the fillet in the cornmeal. Deep-fry or sauté. This makes a beautiful crunchy crust, covering a perfectly tender piece of fish.

A Few Simple Accompaniments . . .

» Lemon always goes well with fried fish.

» Dipping sauce—add fresh herbs (a heaping tablespoon; chives are nice) to 1/2 cup of sour cream, along with a little lemon juice.

» Herb butters work well—add a tablespoon of any fresh herb or a teaspoon of any dried herb (try basil, rosemary, dill, thyme, or tarragon) to half a cup of softened butter, along with a dash of lemon juice, salt and pepper, and a tablespoon of chopped, fresh parsley.

» Make a horseradish butter by adding a tablespoon of prepared horseradish to half a cup of butter (the butters keep well in a cooler).

Corn, Coleslaw, & Potatoes . . .

» Ears of corn can be roasted in the fire. Soak the ears with the husks on in water for about 30 minutes. Snuggle them into the coals right alongside the fire. Cooking usually takes about 30 minutes. Peel back the husks and use the herb butter on the corn.

» A simple but tasty coleslaw—chop cabbage and apples, toss with a little olive oil and some lemon juice. Salt and pepper to taste.

» For sensational baked potatoes—before wrapping each potato in foil, add a crushed clove of garlic. Potatoes cook in a little more than 30 minutes, nestled along the edge of the coals. Turn them frequently.

Chowder, the Other Shorelunch Option...

Another simple, hearty, delicious shorelunch choice is to prepare one of the soups or chowders in this cookbook at home, minus the fish. Chill the soup and take it with you.

In the field, save a portion of the morning's catch, clean it and cut it into one-inch chunks as the soup heats. When it comes to a simmer, add the fish, bring it back to just a simmer, and cook for another 5 to 8 minutes. This is a popular option for anglers out ice-fishing.

» A simple soup or chowder shorelunch, cooked on a Coleman stove and served with rice.

Another Outdoor Chowder Option . . .

This absolutely delicious chowder can be made quickly outdoors without any preparation, except to gather the ingredients.

To serve four...

1 onion, diced (optional)
1 lb. chorizo sausage
four 15-ounce cans of Italian-style diced tomatoes (with Italian seasonings)
one 15-oz. can of chicken broth
1 pound of chunked fish
salt and pepper
Tabasco sauce

» Sauté the sausage and onion in a skillet for several minutes, breaking the sausage apart with a spatula. Add the canned diced tomatoes. Simmer for about 10 minutes, adding a little broth as the mixture reduces. Add fish and continue to cook 5 to 8 minutes more, adding more broth if the chowder gets too thick. Season with salt and pepper and a big splash of Tabasco.

» This is deep in the bush in northwest Ontario, mid-January, with the In-Fisherman staff on a filming excursion for giant lake trout. One small trout was the main course in "Another Outdoor Chowder Option," made quickly over an open fire during a noon break.

Traditional
PAN-FRIED Fish

WITH SAUTÉED FISH as the centerpiece, in the field or at home, substitute the tartar sauce to suit the season and your taste: sweetcorn relish in August or wild rice in the fall, or simple fresh asparagus, lightly steamed and tossed with a lovely herb butter, in spring. This pan-fried fish has a wonderful smoky, salty flavor.

To Serve Four . . .

6 strips thick-cut smoked bacon
3/4 c. flour seasoned with salt and freshly ground white pepper
four 6-oz. fish fillets

» Cut the bacon into 1/4–inch pieces and fry them in a cast-iron skillet until crisp. Remove the bacon and reserve.

» Dredge the fillets in the seasoned flour and sauté them in the hot bacon grease, about 4 minutes per side, until golden brown.

Tartar Sauce...

2 egg yolks
juice of 1 lemon
dash of Tabasco sauce
dash of Worcestershire sauce
1 c. olive oil
1 tsp. Dijon mustard

salt and freshly ground white pepper
1 tbsp. capers
1 tbsp. fresh parsley, chopped
2 tsp. fresh tarragon, chopped
1 tbsp. sweet gherkin pickle, chopped
1 tbsp. black Niçoise olives, pitted and coarsely chopped

» In a blender or food processor with a steel blade, add the egg yolks, mustard, lemon juice, salt, pepper, Tabasco, and Worcestershire sauce and purée about 1 minute.

» While continuing to mix, add the olive oil slowly and steadily, starting with droplets to get a proper emulsion. If it gets too thick, add a few drops of warm water.

» Remove the sauce from the food processor and fold in the chopped gherkin, olives, capers, parsley, and tarragon. Taste and adjust seasoning.

« FISH TIP: Many bass fisheries around North America have too many small bass. In southern waters, where fish grow fast, we often harvest fish up to about 14 inches. In northern waters, fish of about 12 inches are perfect and one of our favorites. Spotted bass (pictured) are another popular table fish.

» COOK'S TIP: The most common question I get about cooking fish is how to tell when it's done—still moist and juicy, but not raw or overcooked. All other rules aside, cut into the thickest part of the fish and take a look. It should be translucent and flake easily.

24-Hour
HASH

A NICE alternative evening meal, in the field or at home—but it really excels as a breakfast or as a midnight snack. Serve it with poached eggs, though sunny-side-up and fried are easier in the field.

To serve four . . .

3 tbsp. butter
8 small-to-medium new potatoes, sliced thin
1 red bell pepper, diced
1 green bell pepper, diced
1 tsp. garlic, chopped
1 red onion, diced
4 fillets, about 6 oz. each, cut into 1-inch cubes
2 fresh tomatoes, peeled, seeded and diced
dash nutmeg
dash balsamic vinegar
1 tbsp. fresh thyme, chopped
1 tbsp. fresh parsley, chopped
8 eggs, if desired, cooked to your preference

» In a heavy skillet, melt the butter until foamy. Over medium heat, add the new potatoes and sauté them until tender and starting to brown, probably about 8 minutes.

» Add the peppers, garlic, and onion and sauté for about 5 minutes, stirring occasionally.

» Add the fish (mild fish like walleye or bass) and cook 5 minutes more, stirring.

» Add the tomatoes, herbs, vinegar, and salt and pepper to taste, and cook 1 minute longer—just to warm last ingredients.

» Divide the mixture onto four plates and top each with a few eggs.

« **FISH TIP:** "Do fish get tougher as they get older?" Yes, but not so much as most land-based animals.

Fish that grow larger as they get older become coarser-fleshed and begin to taste stronger. In particular, strong-tasting fish become even stronger-tasting—sheepshead and white bass, for example. Older and larger fish usually are still adaptable to certain recipes—but these are the fish we usually release. The oldest fishes are the sturgeons, like the lake sturgeon, which can live 75 years.

Fish that remain small and grow older, the case at times with male fish, also become firmer-fleshed. We've had some small, old, male catfish that were tough as an old belt.

Classic Pan-Fried
WALLEYE
with Tartar Sauce & Overnight Coleslaw

HERE'S ANOTHER sauté recipe, plus coleslaw, and an easy tartar sauce. All of this except the fish is prepared in advance to maximize fishing and relaxing time. The ambiance won't be the same, but this is just as good at your dining room table at home.

Dust Mix...

» One part flour mixed with two parts cornmeal, seasoned breadcrumbs (or crushed crackers) and salt and pepper. To serve two, 1/4 cup of flour with 1/2 cup of crumbs will do two 6- to 8-ounce fillets.

» To spice things up, add onion powder, garlic powder, cayenne (to taste), plus paprika for color. Store in a zipper-locking plastic bag.

» Dredge each fillet in the dust mix, gently shaking off any extra. Place in a hot skillet with a coating of butter, oil, or bacon fat. Cook over medium coals.

Easy Tartar Sauce...

Combine:

1 c. mayonnaise
2 tbsp. sweet gherkin pickles, chopped
1 tbsp. capers
1 tbsp. Dijon mustard
1 tsp. fresh parsley, chopped
1 tsp. fresh tarragon, chopped (or 1/2 tsp. dried)
1 tsp. lemon juice
salt and pepper to taste

Overnight Coleslaw...

Dressing:

1 bay leaf
3/4 c. red wine vinegar
3 tbsp. brown sugar
1 clove garlic, crushed
dash of Tabasco
salt and pepper to taste

» Place the ingredients in a saucepan and bring to a boil. Remove from heat and allow the liquid to cool.

Whisk in:

2 tbsp. caraway seed, toasted
1 tbsp. honey
1 tbsp. Dijon mustard
1/2 c. vegetable oil
salt and pepper to taste

Toss dressing with:

1/2 head red cabbage, thinly sliced
1 red onion, thinly sliced

» Marinate overnight.

« **FISH TIP:** Whether on ice or open water, smaller lake trout (2 to 4 pounds) also work well fried for shorelunch. Lake trout weighing up to about 6 pounds work baked in foil or in the alternative recipe that follows this one. The trout must be perfectly fresh. Many other fresh fish, including pike, go well in this recipe.

» **COOK'S TIP:** Many anglers prefer a crustier coating on their fish. Check "My Favorite Dry Breading" on page 100. Make sure your pan is initially very hot, for crispy fish.

BAKED FISH
for a Rainy Day

THIS SIMPLE and versatile recipe is easy to prepare over hot coals. On a rainy day, build your campfire under a tarp to warm up while lunch cooks. If you need to come in and dry off, bake the fish in the oven. I prefer to leave the fish whole, as the bones add flavor and help the fish to retain moisture, but this works well with fillets, as we've shown here. If you know your wild mushrooms, be sure to try our variation. Delicious!

To serve two...

one 2 lb. walleye (or two fillets)
2 tbsp. herb butter
one lemon cut into rounds
salt and pepper
1/4 c. breadcrumbs (if using fillets)
new potatoes
olive oil
1 tbsp. mashed garlic or garlic powder to taste
salt and pepper
fresh or dry herbs

» For a whole fish, scale, gut, and rinse the fish. Place a generous helping of herbed butter in the cavity, sprinkle with salt and pepper, and layer the lemon slices in the fish. Close up the fish and wrap in aluminum foil. Buried in coals, or in a 350°F oven, the fish takes about 10 to 15 minutes to cook.

» For fillets, lay each on a piece of aluminum foil. Smear a generous helping of the butter over the fish, sprinkle with salt, pepper, and the breadcrumbs. Place a few lemon slices on top. If cooking in the coals, cover the fish completely in foil and nestle in the coals and cook for about 10 minutes.

If using an oven, wrap the foil up around the edge of the fillet but leave the top open slightly; cook the same amount of time—about 10 minutes.

» For an added treat, wrap a serving or two of small to medium new potatoes in foil with about 2 tablespoons of olive oil , salt, pepper, garlic, and a sprinkle of herbs. Buried in hot coals, they take about 30 minutes. At home they cook in about 30 minutes at 375°F.

Herb Butter . . .

1/2 lb. butter
juice of 1/2 orange
juice of 1/2 lemon
1/2 tbsp. fresh thyme, marjoram, parsley, or herbs of your choice, chopped fine
salt and pepper to taste

» Mix the ingredients together, using your imagination to adjust the seasonings to fit your taste. Or do a Cajun butter by adding Tabasco and cayenne, or make a red-wine butter by adding a touch of red wine, with shallots and herbs.

» COOK'S TIP: Don't worry—be happy: The only thing that can really go wrong here is if you cremate the fish. Over hot coals there always may be a charred spot or two on the fish, but sometimes that tastes the best. Same with the potatoes.

No herbed butter? This turns out fine with just a pat of plain butter and maybe a splash of wine. No wine? Use beer. No beer? Use a little lemon. No lemon? I never go anywhere without a lemon.

» COOK'S TIP: Another variation—**Baked Fish with Wild Mushrooms**. Per person: One square foot of tin foil generously buttered. Place a fillet on the foil and sprinkle it with 1/2 cup of sliced wild mushrooms (a hen-in-the-woods mushroom is pictured here). Add salt and pepper to taste, plus 1 teaspoon of fresh herbs, chopped. Wrap the fillet in the foil and bake for about 12 minutes at 350°F or bury it in your campfire coals.

CLEANING The Catch

THE ABILITY TO CLEAN the catch with care and precision is a skill born of knowledge and practice. The product you bring to the kitchen affects what appears on the table. A one-pound walleye carefully filleted produces two fillets each weighing about 4 ounces. Lack of precision might reduce those fillets to 3.5 ounces each, a waste.

Without the skill to butterfly fish, several presentation methods suggested in this book may be out of reach; and while not critical, using a butterflied presentation is a unique touch that's visually interesting and fun. So it is with several of the cleaning methods shown. Here, we suggest fundamental cleaning techniques that apply to, or can be adapted to, the recipes in this book.

Tools

The tools needed to clean fish successfully depend on the chosen cleaning method. The skillful fish cleaner knows a variety of methods and uses them depending on the chosen recipe.

For recipes in this book, at the cleaning station should be at least one knife and perhaps several; a fish-dispatching dowel; a bowl of fresh water and ice; and towels to keep the station clean. A sharpening stone and steel should be kept handy too, in case needed. A scaling tool should be on hand, as well as a fish skinner. Many anglers prefer to use an electric knife to fillet fish. We prefer traditional knives but would use an electric knife if the cleaning detail were particularly large.

Basic Tools

⌃ **KNIVES**—If you have only one knife, it should have about a 6-inch blade. Knives with different blade sizes are helpful. Use a 7- or 8-inch blade on larger fish like salmon. Match the knife to the task. A knife with a 4-inch blade does a nice job on panfish. Many electric fillet knives are available with different blade sizes. Anglers who clean large quantities of fish often prefer electric knives.

⌃ **FISH SKINNERS**—The traditional skinner is the handheld pincher design that also works for removing fins. The Townsend Fish Skinner "peels" fish for pan-frying or baking.

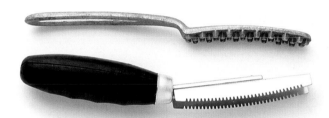

⌃ **STONE AND STEEL**—A stone sharpens blade edges, while steel realigns them. A good knife stays sharp for a long time, but the edge may need realigning (a touch-up) during each cleaning session. Sharpen the typical fillet knife by drawing it at a 15- to 20-degree angle across a fine-grade honing stone. Realign edges by drawing a knife at the same angle over the steel, pulling the knife toward you across the steel. Use the same number of light strokes on each side of the blade.

⌃ **SCALERS**—A scaler can be as simple as a spoon or as advanced as an electric scaler. A spoon or even the edge of a knife works well on easy-to-scale fish like crappies. For walleyes, perch, bluegills, and the like, something with more backbone is necessary. To reduce flying scales, hold the fish under water—in a sink, perhaps—as you scale them. Another option is to scale them inside a paper sack or garbage bag. Pinch the top of the sack shut and give the bag a snap to move the scales to the bottom of the sack.

FILLET BOARD—Plastic fillet boards are durable and easy to keep clean, but traditional wood boards work, too.

⌃ **CLEANING GLOVE**—
Made from the same material as a bullet-proof vest, these gloves can take knife cuts without cutting your hand. This one is from Rapala.

Using a Knife

Knives are built to function like the muscles in your body. Muscular movement begins with larger muscles and progresses to smaller muscles or muscle groups. A hook-set while fishing, for example, begins with the large leg, butt, and back muscles. Then in rapid succession, smaller shoulder and upper arm muscles work and quickly pass the action to the small muscles in the lower arm, hand, and fingers.

Bigger muscles start the work; finer muscles finish it. Larger muscles are for larger, coarser tasks; finer muscles are for smaller, finer tasks. So it is with the design and use of a knife. The thicker butt is designed to handle coarse work, while the finer tip is for finishing work.

Fillet knives should have a heavier butt, tapering progressively into a small point. Fillet knives that taper less progressively are designed for heavier fillet work.

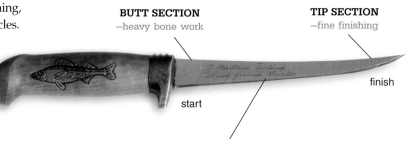

WORKLOAD TRANSFER—Cutting tasks begin with the butt and transfer to the tip for finishing work.

BUTT SECTION —heavy bone work

TIP SECTION —fine finishing

finish

start

MIDDLE SECTION—Determines the primary purpose of the knife. A knife that tapers quickly and progressively toward a fine point is for general cutting purposes, especially on small to medium fish. A knife that doesn't taper progressively but ends quickly with a sharp point is for heavy-duty work.

At the Cleaning Table

At the cleaning table, cleanliness is important. Have ice available for fish that have already been cleaned and to chill fillets from fish still alive when they reach the cleaning table. To fillet our catch, we need:

» Cleaning utensils, including fillet knives and sharpening tools; a fish-dispatching dowel; and a bowl of cold water (add ice) to soak fillets for a short time to remove blood and bacteria.

» Clean paper towels for wiping slime from fish and keeping the fillet board clean. Pat fillets dry after they've soaked if you don't plan to freeze them.

⩘ At the cleaning table.

Procedure

(1) If fish are alive, they should be bled; then dispatch them with a sharp blow to the head with the dowel, just behind the eyes. The dowel is a 15-inch length of one-inch dowel or the handle from a hammer—available in hardware stores.

⌃ Keep the cleaning station and fish as clean as possible.

(2) Remove the fillets. Although it's often difficult and not critical, try not to rupture the digestive tract with your knife.

(3) Place fillets in cold water to help remove blood and bacteria. With lean fish such as catfish, pike, or walleyes, an option is to add 1/2 teaspoon of salt.

(4) Discard the carcass, wipe the board and knife clean, and start on another fish. Replace the water in the bowl when it begins to thicken with fish juices.

Bleeding the Fish

"Bleeding" reduces the amount of blood that needs to be removed from fillets when you clean fish. This results in pearly white, clean-looking fillets that often keep and taste better. Bleeding also keeps the work area clean. Fish must be alive for bleeding to work.

The best way to bleed fish is to insert a knife point into a fish's heart cavity. Move the knife point around just a bit to be sure the heart or a major artery is severed.

Fish can also be bled in the field by gutting them immediately after they're caught and then placing them on ice. If you prefer not to gut fish in the field right after they've been caught, and if they're still going to be placed on ice, bleed them using the above procedure.

We often bleed our fish while they're still in the livewell or in a keep sack once we're home and about to clean the fish. We then put them briefly back into the livewell to bleed out.

Another method for smaller fish is to place them in a 5-gallon bucket and bring this to the cleaning table. Bleed them and place them back in the bucket for a moment. It takes only about 20 seconds for a fish to bleed out.

⌃ Insert a knife point into the fish's heart cavity, either above or below the pectoral fins, depending on the fish species.

Basic Filleting

Filleting is the most popular method for cleaning most fish. The steps are easy but require practice to master.

⌄ Make the initial cut at an angle just behind the pectoral fin. Cut with the scales, not through them. Include as much as possible of the loin, where the neck meets the back of the head.

⌄ Make a stomach cut past the anal fin.

⌄ Cut down to the backbone, lift the dorsal (back) portion of the fish slightly, and turn the knife blade toward the tail of the fish.

⌄ Making certain to use the butt section of the knife to cut through the rib cage, slide the knife along the backbone toward the tail. Lead with the butt of the knife, making sure to cut as close as possible to the backbone so little meat is wasted.

⌄ Remove the rib cage by leading with the butt or middle of the knife and finishing with the middle or tip of the knife. The knife blade should slip just below the ribs, cutting through the epipleural ribs in the process.

⌄ If the fish hasn't been scaled, remove the skin by sliding the blade of the knife between the skin and the fillet. Lead with the butt of the knife, beginning either at the head or tail end of the fillet.

» Once the rib bones are removed, the only thing between you and a totally boneless fillet are the epipleural ribs or pin bones. These are small rib bones that lie at a right angle to the main ribs, along the upper portion of the rib cage.

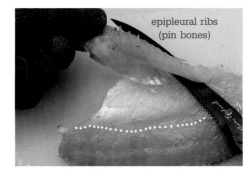

epipleural ribs (pin bones)

Total Bone Removal

Once fish such as walleye, crappies, and stripers are filleted and the rib bones are removed, only a small line of bones remains, called the epipleurals, or "pin" bones. Many people don't find these objectionable in smaller fillets, as the bones can be eaten right along with the rest of the fish, especially when fish are deep-fried or pan-fried. On the other hand, some people object to any bones.

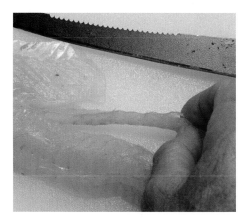

⌃ One way to remove the epipleurals is to make a cut along each side of the bones. This leaves the fillet bone-free.

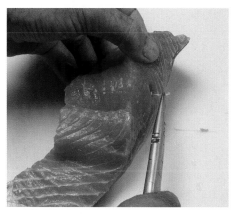

⌃ Another method is to use pliers to grip each individual bone and pull it from the fillet. This works for larger fillets—especially portions of salmon and trout—but is too time-consuming for use with lots of smaller fillets.

⌃ In a butterflied trout or a fish fillet in which the skin remains on the outside of the fillet, make a V-cut on each side of the bones (without cutting through the skin). A small scissors can also be used to trim (remove) the V-cut.

⌃ Perhaps the best method is for the diner to remove the bones at the table and set them aside on the plate. This requires knowing that the bones exist and where they are, not only when presented with a fillet but also when dealing with whole fish.

Pan Dressing

≈ Insert the knife point under the skin at the rear of one side of the dorsal fin.

≈ Slide the knife forward just under the skin, past the front of the dorsal fin. Do this on both sides of the fish.

≈ Use the tip of your knife to cut along the ventral (stomach) portion of the fish, around the anal pore, and along the pelvic fin.

≈ Make a fillet cut in back of the head on each side of the body.

≈ Grab the pelvic fin and pull it forward sharply.

≈ Remove the offal along with the pelvic fin, and remove the head from the fish.

≈ Remove the dorsal fin by pulling from back to front.

≈ If the fish has been scaled, it's pan-ready. If you prefer to skin the fish, peel it with a Townsend Fish Skinner.

≈ The skinned, pan-ready fish.

Gilling and Gutting Trout

⌃ Insert the knife point through the throat or tongue connection.

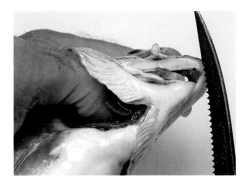

⌃ Cut the throat or tongue connection.

⌃ Insert the knife point in the anal pore and begin cutting forward.

⌃ Run the knife up the stomach lining to the gills.

⌃ Holding the throat connection, pull it toward the rear of the fish to remove the gills and intestines.

⌃ Slit the kidney at the top of the body cavity down the middle for the length of the fish, and scrape it free with your thumb (or use a spoon).

« The cleaned cavity is ready to be stuffed, or the fish can be cooked in any favorite recipe.

Gilling and Gutting Other Fish

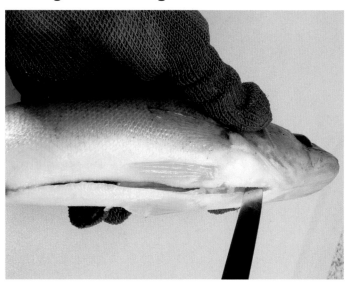

⌃ Run the knife from the anal pore up the stomach lining to the rear of the pectoral fins. Force the knife through this area, cutting forward to the rear of the gill arch.

⌃ Cut through each side of the gill arch region.

⌃ Remove the intestines and other visceral organs. Grip the gills near the rear and separate them from the fish by pulling them forward—toward the mouth of the fish.

⌃ Clean the kidney from the top of the body cavity.

Butterflying

⩘ After scaling the fish (except trout), make a fillet cutting through the ribs but take care not to cut through the belly (ventral) skin.

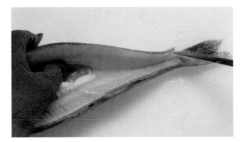

⩘ Finish the fillet cut at the tail on this side, again being careful not to cut through the ventral skin.

⩘ Remove the intestines and stomach.

⩘ Finish the total fillet cut on this side by making a cut behind the fish's head.

⩘ Using the same procedure, remove the fillet from the opposite side.

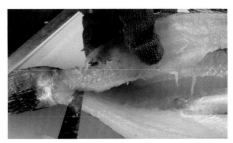

⩘ Make a careful cut below the backbone, beginning at the back of the stomach cavity and continuing to the base of the tail.

⩘ Cut through the skin at the base of the tail and lift the backbone from the fillet.

⩘ Remove the fish's head, along with the backbone.

⩘ Remove the primary ribs. The epipleural ribs can also be removed, being careful once again not to cut through the outer skin.

《 This is the final product ready to be cooked. Butterflying can also be reversed, cutting along each side of the backbone from inside the body cavity of the fish once it's been gilled and gutted.

Steaking and Chunking

⌃ Cut steaks about 1 inch thick from the loin portion of the fish. The loin is the portion of the fish above the rib cage. Remove the belly fat if you prefer.

⌃ Chunk a fillet by cutting it into serving-sized portions.

⌃ The tail portion of the fish can be left whole but is usually filleted.

⌃ Use pliers to grip pin bones and pull them from the fillet.

Y-Bone Removal—One Method

⌃ Once a fillet has been removed, cut straight down and then back to remove the tail section of the fillet. The tail section does not contain bones. Continue to remove sections about 3 inches long. The filleted pieces and skin are shown separated.

⌃ Remove the rib cage and a portion of belly fat from a chunk of fillet.

⌃ This side view shows the approximate position of the Y-bones.

⌃ Find the Y-bones. Look and feel for a line of white bones protruding from the flesh. Placing the knife on the top side of the line of bones, cut straight down until you hit the Y-bones as they bend. Turn your knife toward the top of the fillet portion and continue to cut along the bones.

⌃ After you reach the end of the bones, one option is to cut straight down and remove the top boneless section of loin.

⌃ A distinct crease or cutline runs through the center of the fillet. Insert the knife into that line, cut straight down for about 1/4 inch and then continue to cut toward the top of the fillet. You should feel the Y-bones under the tip of your knife as you continue to cut beneath them.

⌃ The bones are removed, leaving two boneless sections plus the section of Y-bones (held here) to be discarded.

⌃ Another option with larger pike is to remove the Y-bones, leaving the pike portion in one piece.

Y-Bone Removal—Another Method

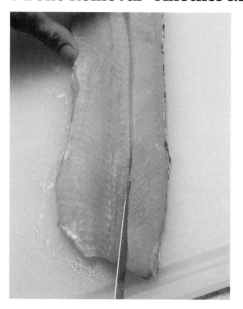

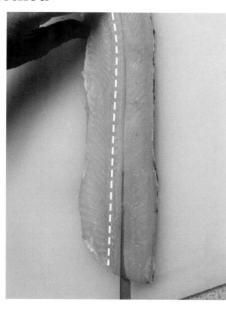

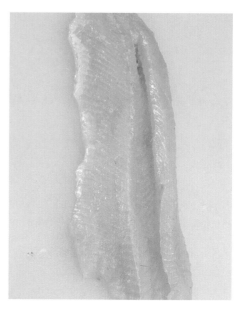

⌃ **ANOTHER METHOD** leaves the fillet in one piece. Once you meet bone on the initial Y-bone cut, continue to cut along the bones until you reach the end of them.

⌃ Now cut below them until you reach the end of the Y-bones.

⌃ Remove them from the fillet. The portion of fillet is intact.

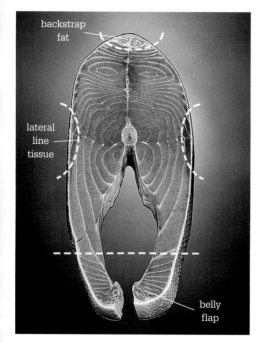

backstrap fat

lateral line tissue

belly flap

Contaminant Concentration

《 The table quality of your catch is influenced by where you fish. For example, algae blooms may affect some lakes and ponds during summer, and some algae species produce chemicals that give fish a muddy or "off" taste. Use an appropriate recipe to cover this flavor.

Many waters harbor contaminants that transfer to fish. Most bodies of water are monitored and health advisories are posted. Use cleaning procedures that reduce the levels of some contaminants, help fish keep longer, and allow them to taste better.

Some contaminants are bound into the fatty belly flaps, backstrap fat, and lateral line tissues. These areas also harbor strong tastes and turn rancid faster than leaner surrounding tissue. Remove these when you can.

Y-Bone Removal—Yet Another Method

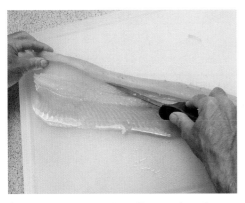
⌃ Use the same technique illustrated on the previous page to cut along the top of the Y-bones. The rib cage has already been removed.

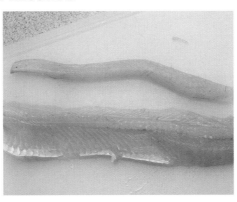
⌃ Remove the top boneless portion of loin.

⌃ Make a cut from the back of the rib cage by inserting the knife in the obvious crease line in the tail portion of the fillet.

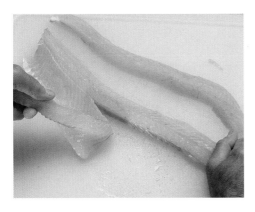
⌃ "Unzip" the bottom portion of the fillet by pulling it forward. This portion is boneless.

⌃ Another boneless portion can be removed by cutting the remaining part of the tail in back of the rib cage (the upper part of the tail above the crease in the fillet).

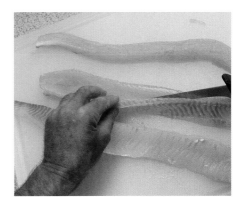
⌃ Cut below the line of Y-bones to remove another small boneless strip.

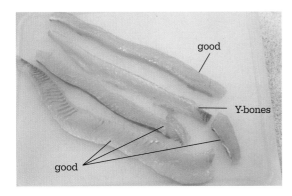
good
Y-bones
good

» Although this is a popular method, most recognize that it uses many more steps to arrive at the same result as the method illustrated on the previous page.

KEEPING The Catch

ALL FRESHWATER FISH have delicate flesh that begins to deteriorate before the fish dies, if it's roughly handled or excessively stressed. Keeping fish lively as long as possible in a good livewell or in a keep sack before cleaning them is one step to fine-tasting fish. Stringers stress fish more than other methods, unless the water's cold. When the water's warm, it's usually best to dispatch fish immediately and surround them with ice.

After death, fish flesh deteriorates quickly if the fish isn't handled correctly. Once they die, gut them immediately when possible to do so. Don't let sour, bacteria-filled stomach and intestinal juices touch the flesh for long. Gutting fish also bleeds them: blood left in flesh speeds deterioration. Wash gutted fish in cold water to remove bacteria, then surround the fish with crushed ice to retard any bacterial growth.

Icing Fish

In the field, icing fish is the best way to keep them fresh once they've been killed and gutted or filleted. Crushed ice works best because it packs more closely, cools more quickly, and keeps fish colder than would blocks of ice or

« Stringers keep fish alive in cold water, if the fish are kept in one place and not dragged in and out of a boat or up and down a bank. Keep fish alive until just before they're cleaned. If they die, immediately gut, gill, and wash them, then transfer them to ice. Other options for keeping fish include livewells, fish baskets (for panfish), and nylon or cloth mesh keep sacks, including duck decoy sacks.

⌃ **STORING FISH IN THE ROUND**—Fish keep fresher longer stored gilled and gutted—in the round—surrounded by ice. This almost doubles the time fish can be kept. Fillet the fish just before you're ready to use them.

frozen bottles of water. So, after gutting the fish, rinse them in cold water and surround them with crushed ice. Don't let fish soak for long—even in icy water.

Use the same strategy with fish at the cleaning table. Unless they're fresh and lively from a livewell, the fish should already be iced. Once a fish is cleaned, immediately immerse it in iced water. Once it's chilled, give it a quick rinse, pat it dry with a towel, wrap it with cling wrap, and surround it with crushed ice. Crushed ice keeps fish for at least five days, although the table quality of the flesh deteriorates slightly each day.

SUPER CHILLING—Wrap fillets and pan-dressed fish (fish in the round) tightly in plastic wrap after they've been patted dry; slip them into individual plastic bags; and layer the fish in the ice chest, making sure to surround each fish with plenty of salted ice. Super-chilling lowers the temperature to just above 32°F. Replenish salted ice as it melts, and be sure the meltwater can drain away.

Super Chilling

This is another method for keeping fish in the field. Super-chilled fish that have been gutted and left in the round can be kept on ice for five days and often longer. Properly stored fillets can be kept for up to five days, although, as we've said, it's best not to fillet fish until you have to.

To super-chill, line the bottom of an insulated cooler with several inches of crushed ice, leaving the drain open. In another container, mix coarse ice cream salt and crushed ice at a ratio of 1 to 20. For average-sized coolers, that's one pound of salt to 20 pounds of ice.

Packaging for the Refrigerator

The temperature of most refrigerators is set at about 40°F. The best way to keep fish in a refrigerator is to turn the thermostat down to almost freezing, but that isn't good for other things in the refrigerator, which may actually freeze.

Another option is to surround the fish with crushed ice. Partially fill a bowl with the ice, wrap the fish tightly in

cling wrap, surround and cover them with ice, then cover the bowl with cling wrap, as well. Drain the melt water frequently so the fish doesn't soak in water. Proper icing lowers the storage temperature to about 34°F, which allows additional days of storage.

If you don't have crushed ice, pat the fish dry with paper towels. Moisten a clean dishtowel and line the bottom of a bowl with it. Spread the fillets on top and cover the bowl with cling wrap. This keeps fillets reasonably cold and moist but not sloppy wet. With this method, fish keep for about 5 days in the round and 3 days filleted. Again, never keep fish in a plastic bag soaking in water and bacteria-prone fish juices.

In the restaurant, Lucia's staff doesn't have crushed ice, so they use ice cubes. They place the fish on a bed of ice cubes, which they put in plastic bags to cover the fish.

STORING IN THE REFRIGERATOR—Fill a bowl half full with crushed ice and place the wrapped fish on the ice. Cover the fish with more ice and cover the bowl with cling wrap. Periodically drain the meltwater. Fish stored in crushed ice (34°F) keep longer than fish stored at typical refrigerator temperatures.

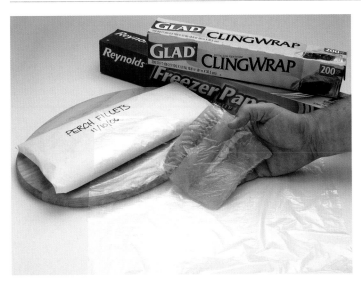

⌃ **FREEZING**—One way to freeze fish is to tightly wrap it in freezer-grade cling wrap. Follow with a secondary wrapping in cling wrap. Finish with wax-coated freezer wrap. Record the contents and packaging date on the outside.

Freezing Fish

Fish flesh loses its quality in the freezer through dehydration and oxidation. "Freezer burn" (whitish leather-tough flesh) is an advanced stage of dehydration. Freezer burn results from using the wrong wrap or wrapping improperly. If your wrap doesn't seal in moisture effectively, fish flesh loses its moisture and turns tough.

Oxidation is a result of poor packaging. Using the wrong wrap or failing to remove air from the package before freezing causes oxygen to combine with polyunsaturated fats and oils in the flesh. These fats turn rancid in the presence of oxygen.

Properly frozen fish keeps well and holds its flavor for months, although the quality deteriorates progressively the longer they're frozen.

Packaging Materials

The objective is to seal in moisture and hold out oxygen. Aluminum foil works, though it punctures easily. It can be used as a final wrap following cling wrap. Polyvinylidene chloride, the material in cling wraps, forms a good barrier and clings to

fish, eliminating air pockets. It's the best initial wrap. Most companies make "freezer grade" cling wraps.

One simple method is to wrap fish in cling wrap, squeezing as much air as possible from the wrap, then follow with another layer of cling wrap (wrapping still tighter and forcing out more air). Finally, add a layer of wax-coated freezer wrap. Write the date frozen, fish type, size, and any other information on the outside of the package.

Zipper-lock "freezer bags" also form a good barrier against air and moisture. Layer a couple of fillets or place a fish in the round in the bottom of a bag. To remove air from the bag, zip almost completely shut and submerge the bag in a water-filled container. Seal the bags underwater. A little water may enter the bag, but that's better than leaving in air.

Vacuum sealing machines, although more expensive than the methods mentioned so far, are available and add a professional touch to the freezing process.

Freezing in Water

Commercially frozen fish often are glazed with a coating of ice to protect the flavor and table quality. It takes freezer temperatures of about -40°F to accomplish this. Water can be used to store fish in other ways.

Disagreement exists about whether or not the methods that follow are advisable. Our practical experience over the years is that lean fish like walleyes and pike retain their flavor well when a little water is used in the freezing process. We don't use water with fish like salmon and trout.

One method is to pack fish tightly in lidded plastic containers and fill the containers almost to the brim with water. Use enough water to cover the fish, but don't leave large empty spaces for water—too much water draws nutrients from the fish, causes the fish to freeze more slowly, and crushes them when the water freezes.

Pack the container with as much fish as possible, minimizing empty spaces. Then seal the remaining spaces with water. If fish portions protrude from the ice after freezing, add a little more water and refreeze.

Another method that works well is to layer fish in a freezer-grade plastic locking bag, then add just a little water.

▲ FREEZING—One method is to pack fish tightly in lidded plastic containers and fill the containers almost to the brim with water.

▲ FREEZING—Place fish in a freezer bag, add just a little water, zip the bag almost shut and fold it over the fish, forcing air out until water leaks from the bag. Seal immediately.

Zip up the bag, leaving only a tiny opening. Squeeze the remaining air from the bag by folding the bag over the fish, until a little water just begins to run out. Immediately seal the bag. This simple method is perhaps our favorite method for freezing lean fish fillets.

Freezing Tips

» Divide cleaned fish into serving-sized portions to eliminate leftover thawed fish.

» Freezing breaks down cell walls, the reason frozen fish is less firm than fresh fish and more "weepy." Don't refreeze thawed fish.

» The faster fish freezes, the better. Place packages in the coldest part of a freezer and don't overload the freezer with food to be frozen. Keep the temperature at 0°F or below while the freezing is taking place.

» Thawing fish at room temperature lets thawed parts deteriorate as other parts thaw. Instead, thaw frozen fish in the refrigerator, allowing 24 hours for a 1-pound package. Another option is to place frozen fish in cold water until it's thawed. Keep it in the vapor-proof wrapping as it thaws.

Cooking Tips for Frozen Fish

» To pacify strong flavors added by freezing, soak fish in milk for 15 to 30 minutes before preparation—don't rinse before dusting or using other preparations.

» Seasonings help frozen fish, so add dried herbs to any flour or cornmeal coatings, and consider using bacon fat to sauté. A good wine helps when poaching frozen fish. Consider stronger sauces, especially with stronger-tasting fish like white bass and freshwater drum.

» Frozen fish is never as firm as fresh fish, so it goes well with something crunchy on the plate, like sautéed vegetables, placing the fish on top of the bed of vegetables.

Nutrient and Caloric Values of Some Fish

Fish are nutritious—high in vitamins, minerals, and protein, and low in calories and fat. Research shows that increasing the amount of fish in the diet reduces cholesterol levels and the risk of heart attack.

Fish	Calories	% Protein	% Fat	Sodium (mg)	Fish	Calories	% Protein	% Fat	Sodium (mg)
Burbot (eelpout, lawyer)	80	17	0.9	—	Salmon (Coho)	148	21	6.6	—
Carp	125	17	5.9	44	Shrimp	86	20	0.4	155
Catfish	119	18	5.2	60	Smelt	86	17	3.9	80
Clams	63	11	1.7	190	Suckers	—	21	1.8	53
Cod	74	17	0.5	67	Tuna	122	24	2.2	76
Flounder	88	18	1.4	54	Walleye	89	19	1.5	—
Freshwater Drum (Sheepshead)	—	17	5.5	—	Whitefish	121	19	5.2	52
Haddock	77	18	0.5	98	**Other Common Foods**				
Halibut (Pacific)	119	19	4.3	71	Beef Steak	266	17	26	61
Herring (Lake)	—	19	3.3	—	Beef Liver	141	22	5	33
Lake Trout	169	17	11.1	43	Pork	298	17	24.7	60
Northern Pike	—	19	1.2	52	Chicken	127	23	7	—
Oysters (Eastern)	68	8	1.8	160	Lamb	186	15	13.5	52
Perch (Yellow)	85	19	1.1	63	Cheddar Cheese (1 oz.)	113	7.1	9.1	198
Rainbow Trout	154	21	6.8	43	Egg (1)	80	6	6	70
Salmon (Chinook)	182	18	11.6	42	Whole Milk (1 cup)	159	8	8.5	122

These calculations for 3½-ounce food portions were made by Jeff Gunderson of the Minnesota Sea Grant Institute. Adapted from information supplied by the National Marine Fisheries Service and *Nutritive Value of American Foods in Common Units*, U.S. Department of Agriculture. Agriculture Handbook No. 456, 1975, by Jeff Gunderson for *Fixin' Fish*, University of Minnesota Press, 1984.

Fat Content and Storage Life

When frozen properly, fish with low fat content hold their flavor well for as long as 6 months. Be sure, however, to remove their fatty areas before packaging them.

Species	Storage Time
Lake trout, rainbow trout, whitefish, carp, catfish, ciscoes, smelt, pike	3 to 5 months
Suckers, chinook salmon, coho salmon, white bass	5 to 8 months
Walleyes, yellow perch, bass, burbot, crappies, bluegills	8 to 12 months

When frozen, fish with high fat content generally become rancid more quickly than do lean fish. Exceptions include ciscoes, smelt, and pike, which may not withstand frozen storage as well as other fish of similar fat content. On the other hand, king and coho salmon with their relatively high fat content store better than fish with less fat. Always keep your freezer as cold as possible.

Source: *Fixin' Fish*, University of Minnesota Press.

CHEF Lucia Watson

CHEF LUCIA WATSON owns Lucia's, one of the Twin Cities' favorite restaurants, a cozy, friendly neighborhood establishment in the Uptown section of Minneapolis.

The continuing popularity of Lucia's over the past two decades is a tribute to her sensibility in menu selection and food preparation. She insists on the finest fresh organic ingredients from local and regional purveyors, resulting in a menu vibrant with ever-changing seasonal selections. Lucia's isn't trendy but is always in touch with trends, allowing it to be always contemporary. As a complement to the food, the service at Lucia's is consistently gracious.

Lucia has been honored with many awards over the years and her recipes have been featured in a host of regional and national magazines. Three times in recent years she has been nominated for a James Beard Foundation Award—Best Chef in the Midwest. The Institute for Agriculture and Trade Policy recently honored her with a Commitment to Community Award for her work with local farmers and youth. She is also co-author with Beth Dooley of *Savoring the Seasons of the Northern Heartland*,

> A nice one to be released!

in hardcover from Alfred A. Knopf and in paperback from the University of Minnesota Press.

Chef Watson has been an *In-Fisherman* columnist since 1990. A lifelong angler who once guided in the Boundary Waters Canoe Area, she's just as much at home cooking over an open fire in the wilderness as she is in her restaurant kitchen. She has appeared on In-Fisherman television segments, cooking fish in her restaurant and preparing shore-lunches in the field.

Lucia's restaurant is at 1432 West 31st Street in Minneapolis, 612/825-1572 or visit *lucias.com*. The main restaurant has seating for 60, and the adjoining wine bar seats about 20. There's outdoor seating in summer. Lucia's To Go, her bakery and take-home service, adjoins the bar and restaurant.

« Catching channel catfish for an In-Fisherman Television segment.

TASTE Tempters

FOR OVER 30 YEARS, each issue of *In-Fisherman* magazine has been devoted to teaching anglers how to catch fish—not just a select few species, though *In-Fisherman* readers surely also have their favorites, but everything that swims. In the catching, as in our approach to the eating of fish, the magazine celebrates each species and is thoroughly intrigued with understanding them as well as catching and conserving them. Selective Harvest, described in the opening section of this book, is at the heart of what In-Fisherman is all about. When the right fish

« *In-Fisherman* magazine rests distinctively on newsstands eight times a year throughout North America and is read by some 280,000 subscribers.

are harvested, we can continue a tradition of eating fish because the resource is renewable.

While the magazine remains focused on instruction about how to catch fish, it has also evolved over the years to capture the lifestyle of the exceptional multispecies angler. The reader finds environmental and industry perspectives, science reviews, plus advice on where to go to find the finest fishing and the best fishing vacation spots. Columns also offer humor and reflective essays. It is in this mix that a Taste Tempters column celebrating cooking the catch with distinction fits so naturally.

More information on *In-Fisherman* magazine and the many other aspects of what In-Fisherman does, including its various television programs, is available by visiting *in-fisherman.com*.

⌃ On a summer day in Minneapolis, the three principles involved in creating the Taste Tempters column, In-Fisherman Editor In Chief Doug Stange, Chef Lucia Watson, and Photographer Chuck Nelson, relax in the outside dining area of Lucia's Wine Bar.

« A typical Taste Tempters column is offered in a two-page-spread format, offering a simple but distinctive recipe and compelling photography.

INDEX